CARIBBEAN FLAVORS
for Every Season

85 Coconut, Ginger, Shrimp, and Rum Recipes

BRIGID WASHINGTON
Foreword by **NINA COMPTON**

Skyhorse Publishing

Skyhorse Publishing books may be purchased in bulk at special discounts for sales promotion, corporate gifts, fund-raising, or educational purposes. Special editions can also be created to specifications. For details, contact the Special Sales Department, Skyhorse Publishing, 307 West 36th Street, 11th Floor, New York, NY 10018 or info@skyhorsepublishing.com.

Skyhorse® and Skyhorse Publishing® are registered trademarks of Skyhorse Publishing, Inc.®, a Delaware corporation.

Visit our website at www.skyhorsepublishing.com.

10 9 8 7 6 5 4 3 2 1

Library of Congress Cataloging-in-Publication Data is available on file.

Cover design by David Ter-Avanesyan
Cover photograph by Immanuel Keester

Print ISBN: 978-1-5107-7053-9
Ebook ISBN: 978-1-5107-7150-5

Printed in China

For my mother, Anne Marie Ransome, the definition of self-sacrifice. If I inherit any of your traits, may it be your unfailing love for others and your grace under pressure.

And for Professor Dick J. Reavis, thank you for teaching me to discipline my writing and to believe in the power of journalistic persistence.

CONTENTS

Photograph © Elsa Hahne

FOREWORD

Growing up in the Caribbean, I think, was the best schooling as a chef. Most people have gardens, so farm-to-table is the way of life. There are numerous street vendors selling fruits and vegetables along the road—it's the island grocery store, and you can't beat that. My fondest memory of growing up there was eating very sweet oranges at the beach during a family outing . . . I remember dipping the orange in the salt water; the combination of sweet and salty blew my mind. Or walking through the market and smelling all the fresh spices, such as cinnamon and bay leaves, perfume the air. The open markets in the Caribbean are such a beautiful sight for colorful fruit, vegetables, and fresh fish and butchered meats. Seeing and hearing people interact with their favorite local vendors contributes to the atmosphere as they joke, make mischievous comments, and catch up with one another, since everyone is so familiar. People in the Caribbean have so much history and each island is able to tell their own story through food. The many influences from early settlers such as English, French, Spanish, Indian, Dutch, and African, are interwoven through the islands—each sings its own individual song, but together make a beautiful harmony.

This book brings all of the above together. It expresses the fun, playful way of Caribbean people, along with the different cultures. Reading this book, I can taste the bright, bold flavors of these dishes. Rum is such a big part of the culture in the islands, and Brigid finds intricate ways to incorporate it into many recipes. Coconut is one of those ingredients that is used in a variety of ways in the Caribbean diet, whether using it as a cooking oil in savory applications, or in a sweet dessert, this a staple in our cooking. This book is fun and approachable, and really brings Caribbean cooking to the forefront where it belongs. Hopefully while cooking from this book, you are sipping on some delightful, aged rum!

—Nina Compton, *Top Chef* runner up & fan favorite,
owner & executive chef of New Orleans restaurant Compère Lapin

INTRODUCTION

Within the span of eighty recipes, borders are breached for you, the enterprising home cook. This book brims with relevant, upbeat, and deceptively simple ways you can marry the mouthwatering bounty of the four seasons to the bright flavors of the Caribbean table.

In writing this book, it became apparent that the greatest tragedy of Caribbean cuisine is misconception. Too often the food of the islands is translated to American restaurant tables as simple, fruit-forward fare; these tourist-friendly dishes portray a shallow concept of the West Indies' rich and enduring culinary history. The narrative of the Caribbean is best told through the unfurled flags of the countries that once colonized the region. The settlers from those countries—both indigenous and conquistadors—translated their cuisines into a tradition, honing in on the wonts of their past whilst simultaneously bucking them to befit their new locale.

What happened next was probable. The island nations cultivated their distinct social norms and cash crops in ways that still strongly demark the socio-economic and cultural identity of each isle. The ill-fated identity of slavery and the burns of sugar were bonds of historical proportions. And even though time and technology have advanced the Caribbean agenda—far beyond tourism—each island remains forever fused to the others, largely by traditions of a bygone era. But there remains a special brand of magic found in the islands—its people, and especially its food.

For you, I have written this book to be an approachable, buttoned-down way to incorporate an often misrepresented yet vibrant cuisine with the seasonal fare you already adore. The mezze, Roasted Cauliflower Coconut Tabbouleh, for instance, is equal parts delight and discovery. This recipe traces a path to the Mideast, making the cauliflower the star ingredient and without the use of fussy, far-flung ingredients.

In writing this book, I watched how old memories and recipes came to life beneath my fingers, connecting my past as a child and teenager in Trinidad & Tobago to my present life as a wife and mother of two in Raleigh, North Carolina. If nothing else, this project is a work of syncretism, integrating two worlds, through four ingredients. Within these pages, my goal is to elevate and celebrate the bounty of each American season in a way that salutes the taste of the tropics. And doing so requires a triage of, in my opinion, the most essential West Indian ingredients: coconuts, ginger, shrimp, and rum.

This cookbook offers energetic, easy-to-prepare recipes that celebrates the power of produce while gently connecting it to the flavors of the Caribbean. Crowd-pleasers like Mojito Marinated Veggie Kabobs, Boozy Coconut Bread Pudding, and Grilled Stone

Fruit with Piña Colada Fondue, becomes back-pocket phenomes, as they incorporate familiar ingredients in ingenious yet simple new ways. If you're looking for new ways to create exciting, unique dishes with seasonal produce, this cookbook is for you.

Early on, I realized my culinary curiosity was linked to my upbringing in Trinidad and Tobago. As a child, my mother taught me about the wonder of diversity; one that is an inextricable part of the country to which I belonged. I saw how salient the food-ways of Africans, East Indians, Spanish, Chinese, French, Syrians, Portuguese, and Germans coalesced and gently infiltrated our day-to-day lives. Our dinners were edible geography; from East Indian dahlpuri roti to West African yams. And that was the norm throughout Trinidad & Tobago and throughout the Caribbean. Island folk ate in a way that honored the cultures that formed the region and also in a way that complemented the ebb and flow of their physical environment. It was this intuitive relationship with food and how it shapes my sense of place that drove me to pursue it purely and professionally.

My time at the Culinary Institute of America formalized my rough understanding of food as it pertains to the cultures of yesteryear and the economies of today. It was in the dignified kitchens of the Hyde Park campus where I learned the scope—as well as tedium and toil—that is the business of food. Quick, accurate knife-cuts and rote recollection of cooking ratios boosted my muscle memory in ways I never thought possible. I became a disciplined cook, simply because it was expected of me. And surprisingly enough, I enjoyed the romance of the routine. By way of being Editor in Chief of CIA's monthly publication, I reported on the shape-shifting nature of the industry, interviewing some of its most formidable gatekeepers. At that time, I didn't know these encounters would lead me to this project. I knew with certainty that my experiences would eventually lead me home, but I didn't know it would be via a cookbook, where I would write the story of home.

From my first taste of from-the-nut coconut water as a toddler in South Trinidad to writing this book, all of my experiences have been part of a powerful education. This knowledge of the salience of community, the rhythm of the seasons, and the indomitable healing nature of simple ingredients, will forever form the core my approach to food and life. Because, I wasn't just raised in the Caribbean—but rather, the Caribbean raised me.

I hope you enjoy these recipes and a taste of the islands, from my heart to your kitchen.

—Brigid Washington

A NOTE ON INGREDIENTS

It is no act of happenstance that certain foods render what our bodies need at very specific times of the year. High water content produce like tomatoes, cucumber, and zucchini keep us cool and hydrated during the balmy summer months. The robust, sweet, and starchy products of fall and winter—beets, yams, pumpkins—empower our bodies to tackle the back-breaking chill of winter. And likewise, the verdant green of spring found in snap peas, asparagus, and ramps, whets our appetites for new life that has finally broken ground. When we listen to nature and allow our bodies to hone in on the fleeting flavors of each season, we do ourselves—and the earth—immense good. These recipes reflect a commitment to seasonality. And these four namesake ingredients loosely tether the bounty of each season to the West Indies, in innovative and auspicious ways.

COCONUT

With a litany of derivatives such as water, oil, meat, flour, and sugar, the coconut stands alone as one of the few foods that can be wholly characterized as a superfood. Coconut oil is one of the few non-animal sources of saturated fat, and the presence of lauric acid raises the HDL (the good type of) cholesterol (lauric acid is converted in the body into a compound called monolaurin, which is an antiviral and antibacterial known to destroy a variety of disease-causing organisms). Because coconut water contains high levels of potassium it is oftentimes cited as being a natural electrolyte-rich hydrator. Coconut milk is made from the grated flesh of the nut, which is then soaked in water and strained. The resulting creamy white liquid is coconut milk. This plant-based milk is rich in fiber and vitamins C, E, B1, B3, B5, and B6 and minerals including iron, selenium, sodium, calcium, magnesium, and phosphorous. Unlike cow's milk, coconut milk is lactose-free so it can be used as a milk substitute by those with intolerance to lactose.

GINGER

This firm, gnarled, tan-skinned root has been dubbed, many times over, as one of the world's healthiest foods. And here are some reasons why it lives up to the hype. It almost completely relieves gastrointestinal distress caused by motion sickness, and owing to its anti-inflammatory properties it is used to prevent symptoms of nausea and vomiting in pregnant women. In addition the active compound in the root, gingerols—also the one that gives its distinctive pungent flavor—inhibits the growth of colorectal cancer cells. The versatility of this root does not wane as steeping half an inch of the root in hot water promotes "healthy sweating" during cold and flu season.

SHRIMP

This versatile seafood is arguably one of the lowest in mercury, a likely reason why many people who hold a distaste for seafood happily indulge in shrimp. There is also a very negligible amount of fat, but significant amounts of the minerals phosphorus, magnesium, potassium, and zinc. In addition, this low-calorie crustacean (one medium shrimp contains roughly seven

calories) is also very high in protein, while being low in carbohydrates. And even though most animal protein aren't necessarily synonymous with being pillars of antioxidants, shrimp is high in the mineral selenium. Selenium plays a key role in metabolism and its antioxidant properties protect cells from damage.

RUM

The Caribbean and parts of Latin America produces the vast majority of rum, globally. A byproduct of sugar refining, rum—derived from fermented molasses—was discovered by 17th century plantation slaves. This first branded spirit has proven to be a remedy for peripheral artery disease. Rum helps to restrict the formation of artery blockage; it also acts as a blood thinner and has been known to increases the good type of cholesterol (HDL). In addition, rum is widely used to ease Intermittent Claudication, or muscle pain. At times, osteoporosis (brittle bone disease) is kept at bay, because rum is said to increase the bone mineral density. As an anti-microbial, rum aids those suffering from the common cold as it provides a soothing and warming effect.

A few tidbits that will prove useful when making the recipes:

- Salt and pepper are listed in most every recipe. For brevity, salt is always (always) Kosher, and pepper is coarse ground black pepper.

- There is not tremendous mention of vinegars, but when purchasing a vinegar, the age-old adage of "buy cheap, buy twice" is appropriate. Always use a vinegar you respect.

- Cold lemons are easier to grate and zest, but room temperature lemons release more juice.

- Peeling ginger is easiest with the back of a spoon.

- Where possible, use full-fat coconut milk.

- The shells of shrimp & lobster should be frozen and not discarded, since they will provide you an easy fish stock.

SPRING

Nature's Opening Act

Light Fare

Rhubarb Ginger Challah / 2

Coconut Quinoa Bean Salad / 4

Coconut, Ginger, and Chia Seed
Cluster Granola / 5

Cajun Shrimp & Greek Yogurt
Cornbread / 6

Green Mango Salad / 8

Mains

Bi-Color Cabbage "Tacos" with Grilled
Shrimp & Coconut Green Goddess
Dressing / 9

Grilled Shrimp Skewers with Coconut
Old Bay Aioli / 10

Szechuan Ginger Stir Fry / 11

Garlicky Parmesan Shrimp & Fava
Bean Ravioli with Spinach Almond
Pesto / 12

Shrimp Salade Nicoise with Roasted
Pineapple Vinaigrette / 14

Shrimp, Ginger, and Scallion
Lettuce Wraps / 16

Lobster Sunomono / 17

Creole Bouillabaisse / 18

Spring Pea & Ginger Risotto / 19

Rum-Buttered "Rockaway"
Jerk Wings / 20

Rosemary & Lemon Brick Chicken / 22

To Sip

Bacon, Shrimp, and Jalapeño Bloody
Mary / 24

Knight & Bishop / 26

Sweet Endings

Old School Bananas Foster / 27

Coconut Layer Cake / 28

Rhubarb Ginger Challah

Serves 4

Robust Jewish custom, as well as traditions from many Eastern European nations, has galvanized the culinary position of braided, egg-enriched bread, the world over. It's a relevant icon of both religious and of nationalistic roots. And its laquer-like golden crust and pillowy-soft interior allow for myriad adaptations, like this one. Here, a compote is made by the slow simmer of Springtime rhubarb alongside ginger, spices, and sugar. Through braiding, ribbons of this compote are incorporated into the dough and the result is a showstopper of a loaf, delicious enough to be devoured in seconds. But in that (rare) moment when patience prevails and there are leftovers, day-old challah makes for the best French toast, which naturally you'll serve with a spread of Rhubarb Ginger compote.

FOR THE CHALLAH
2¼ teaspoons active dry yeast
⅓ cup honey, divided
⅔ cup warm water
⅓ cup olive oil
3 eggs + 1 yolk (reserve the white for the egg wash)
2 teaspoons salt
4 cups all-purpose flour

FOR THE COMPOTE
5 medium stalks (about 3 cups) rhubarb, cubed into 1-inch pieces
1 cup white sugar
¼ cup ginger, finely chopped
½ cup water
2 pieces of cloves

Utilizing the bowl of an electric stand mixer, whisk the yeast and 1 teaspoon honey into warm water and allow it to stand for a few minutes until it appears foamy. Add and combine the remaining honey, olive oil, and 2 eggs. Add the salt and flour, and using the dough hook attachment on low speed, mix until the dough begins to come together, about 6–9 minutes. Ready an olive oil–coated bowl. After the dough has come together, place in the oiled bowl and cover with plastic wrap. Allow to rest and rise for a little over an hour, until the dough has doubled in size.

Make the Compote: In a small saucepan over medium heat, combine the rhubarb, sugar, ginger, water, and cloves. Allow the mixture to cook for about 12–15 minutes until the rhubarb begins to soften, and its texture completely melts into a compote. Reduce heat and allow to simmer for 5 minutes until the mixture is thick and viscous. Remove from heat allow to cool and set aside.

Making & Braiding Challah: When the dough has doubled in size, turn it out onto a floured surface and divide in half. Roll the first half of the dough out, so that it resembles a wide rectangle. Spread the rhubarb compote evenly over the surface of the dough, leaving a finger's breadth of space between the rhubarb and the edge of the dough. Roll the dough into a long, tight log, alternating between gently stretching and rolling. The filling should be trapped inside, however, there are worse things than some compote escaping. When it is completely rolled, stretch the compote-filled log as wide and long as you possibility can without compromising the structural integrity. Cut the log in half. Repeat with the remaining dough and filling.

Arrange two ropes in each direction, horizontally and vertically, so that the dough resembles a tight pound sign or hashtag. Braid them so that one side is over the other and under the next. Continue this process, with each strand of the dough rope, until each part is completely interwoven into the next. Tuck the extra odd pieces under the dough. Using your hands, guide the dough into a circular shape.

Use one egg and the remaining egg white to make an egg wash; beat until smooth. Place the challah on a sheet pan covered with a Silpat or parchment paper, and brush the challah with the egg wash. Allow the challah to rise for another hour. Preheat oven to 375°F 15 minutes to the hour. Prior to baking, apply one more coating of egg wash and bake for 40 minutes. Demonstrating an uncanny ability of restraint, attempt to cool on a wire rack, prior to serving.

Coconut Quinoa Bean Salad

Serves 4-6

Don't let the humble preparation of this powerhouse salad deceive you. It's an ideal anytime accompaniment, and a health-conscious respite to your typical starch-heavy sides. Served either warm or room temperature, this colorful salad fuels you with protein, potassium, and essential b-vitamins.

1 cup quinoa, well rinsed
2 tablespoons coconut oil
¼ cup lemon juice
Salt & pepper
¼ cup red onion, chopped
½ cup parsley, chopped
½ cup celery leaves, chopped
1 can black beans, drained
1 can garbanzo beans, drained
1 can red kidney beans, drained

In a large pot on medium high heat, bring two quarts of water to a boil. Add the quinoa and allow to cook uncovered for 10–15 minutes. Most of the water should be absorbed and the quinoa should be light. If you want to serve this salad warm, do not rinse with cold water. Using a fine mesh sieve, strain the quinoa and shake the sieve to remove excess water.

In a large bowl, whisk together the oil, lemon juice, salt, pepper, red onion, parsley, and celery leaves. Add all beans and stir to combine. Add the quinoa and stir. Allow to sit for 10–15 minutes before serving.

Coconut, Ginger, and Chia Seed Cluster Granola

Serves 2-4

This recipe, adapted from food media behemoth the New York Times, *gives an inspired and egg-less way to replicate the elusive clusters found in store-bought granola, at home. Featured here are elements that, on their own, don't necessarily wow; but as they rally under the luscious viscosity of the coconut milk, maple syrup, and coconut oil, produce a gift-worthy pantry staple that surely is the only granola recipe you'll ever use.*

⅓ cup raw coconut oil
⅔ cup maple syrup
½ cup brown sugar
⅔ cup coconut milk
1 teaspoon sea salt
1 teaspoon vanilla extract
½ teaspoon ginger extract
5 cups old fashioned rolled oats, divided
1 cup unsweetened coconut flakes
1 teaspoon ground ginger
¼ cup fresh ginger root, minced
1 cup slivered almonds
⅓ cup chia seeds

Preheat oven to 325°F and line two baking sheets with parchment paper. Over medium heat, bring to a low simmer the coconut oil, maple syrup, sugar, coconut milk, and salt. When the sugar is dissolved, stir in the extracts and allow to slightly cool.

In a food processor, grind 1¼ cups of the oats and ¼ cup of the coconut flakes into a flour. Transfer to a large bowl and stir in remaining oats, coconut, gingers, nuts, and chia seeds. Pour the maple syrup mixture over and stir to combine. Allow this raw granola to sit for 10 minutes.

Using your hands, drop the oat mixture onto the prepared baking sheets and pinch together to form clumps.

Bake for 40–50 minutes, flipping the mixture every 15 minutes very tenderly, so as not to break up the clusters. The granola will be golden brown when it's completed and will continue to carry-over cook as it cools. Allow it to cool on a wire rack. Store in an airtight container for up to one month.

Cajun Shrimp & Greek Yogurt Cornbread

Serves 3–5

Chunks of shrimp are studded throughout this lightened-up (cue the yogurt) comfort-food classic.

1 teaspoon lemon juice
2 cloves garlic, minced
2 teaspoons salt
1 teaspoon black pepper
½ teaspoon paprika
½ teaspoon red pepper flakes
1 cup shrimp, peeled, deveined,
    chopped into thirds
1 tablespoon butter, divided
¼ teaspoon tomato paste
1 cup yellow cornmeal

½ cup all-purpose flour
2 teaspoons baking powder
½ teaspoon salt
¼ teaspoon baking soda
1 egg
1 cup plain Greek yogurt
½ cup whole milk
¼ extra-virgin olive oil
1 tablespoon honey
¼ cup fresh chives, chopped

For the Shrimp: Combine the lemon juice, garlic, salt, black pepper, paprika, and red pepper flakes. Add in the shrimp and allow it to marinate for a few minutes. In a sauté pan, melt half the butter until slightly fragrant. Add the shrimp and then the tomato paste and cook until the shrimp is pink and no longer blue, about 5 minutes. Set aside.

For the Cornbread: Preheat oven to 400°F. With the remaining butter, grease an 8-inch cast iron skillet and place the empty skillet in the oven, as the oven preheats. In a large bowl, combine all the dry ingredients. In another bowl, combine the wet ingredients and stir using a fork, which will help break up the clumps in the yogurt. Using a rubber spatula, add the wet ingredients to the dry ingredients and incorporate. Next, add the chives and the shrimp. Carefully remove the cast-iron skillet from the oven and place the batter into the hot skillet—it should sizzle upon contact. Bake for 16–20 minutes. Serve warm.

Green Mango Salad

Serves 2-4

Fast, fresh, and wildly exotic, this made-in-minutes side salad adds lively bite and refreshing notes to most any meaty main.

2 cloves garlic, minced
1 teaspoon chili flakes
Juice of 2 limes
2 tablespoons Nuoc Nam or fish sauce
1 tablespoon liquefied coconut oil
2 tablespoons agave nectar
2 green mangoes, peeled
¼ cup red onion, sliced thin
¼ cup cilantro, roughly chopped

In a small bowl, strongly whisk the garlic, chili flakes, lime juice, fish sauce, oil, and agave until it is well combined and somewhat emulsified. Set aside.

Using a vegetable peeler, shave the meat off the mango, until you've reached the core. Discard the core and place the mango slices and red onion into the bowl with the dressing. Toss to coat. Season to taste and garnish with cilantro.

Bi-Color Cabbage "Tacos" with Grilled Shrimp & Coconut Green Goddess Dressing

Serves 4

Early spring yields a crop of cabbage that is tight, crisp, and aromatic. Without struggle, it replaces the wheat-dense tortilla for a new kind of shrimp taco.

1 tablespoon extra-virgin olive oil
½ teaspoon cumin
¼ teaspoon red pepper flakes
5 cloves garlic, finely minced
1 pound shrimp, peeled and deveined
Juice of 2 limes, divided
1 cup coconut milk
2 tablespoons agave
¼ cup Greek yogurt
¼ cup coconut oil
¼ cup cilantro, chopped
¼ cup parsley, chopped
½ jalapeño (seeds and ribs removed), finely chopped
4 whole green cabbage leaves
4 whole red cabbage leaves
Handful of fresh pea shoots

Over medium heat, add olive oil to stove-top grill pan or sauté pan. Combine the cumin, chili flakes, and garlic in a large bowl and add the shrimp. Toss to coat the shrimp in the spices. Grill the shrimp for 2 minutes per side. Remove from heat and drizzle with half of the lime juice.

There are two ways to make the dressing. Here's how to do it by hand: In a large bowl combine the milk, agave, yogurt, and coconut oil and whisk until well incorporated. Add the cilantro, parsley, the remainder of the lime juice, and jalapeños, and stir until evenly combined. By machine: Combine all the ingredients in the blender. Blend until completely smooth.

The dressing can be kept refrigerated in an airtight jar for 7 days.

To Assemble: Arrange the cabbage leaves on a plate and spoon shrimp into cabbage cups. Top with peas shoots and then drizzle with coconut green goddess dressing. Serve.

Grilled Shrimp Skewers with Old Bay Aioli

Makes 3 Skewers

It is impossible to bemoan the appeal of grilled jumbo shrimp, especially when they're smeared with an aioli made with seafood's most iconic accompaniment.

1 tablespoon extra-virgin olive oil
Zest and juice of 1 large lemon
3 large cloves garlic, finely minced
1 tablespoon + 2 teaspoons Old Bay
  seafood seasoning
1 teaspoon red pepper flakes

2 teaspoons salt
1 teaspoon black pepper
12 pieces jumbo (16/20) shrimp,
  peeled, deveined, and tails removed
½ cup full-fat mayonnaise
2 teaspoons lemon juice

In a medium-sized bowl, whisk to combine the olive oil, lemon zest and juice, garlic, 1 tablespoon Old Bay, chili flakes, salt, and pepper. Delicately toss the shrimp in the marinade. Set aside for 10 minutes. Meanwhile, make the Aioli. In a small bowl, fiercely whisk the mayonnaise, lemon juice, and 2 teaspoons of Old Bay.

To make the skewers: If utilizing wooden skewers, soak them in water for 1 minute to prevent burning. Then alternate the position of each piece of marinated shrimp on the skewer allowing for the bottom end of one piece to face the top of the other, so that two pieces of shrimp look like one circle. Continue this process for all the shrimp.

Place the shrimp on a wickedly hot indoor stove-top grill pan, or on an equally hot outdoor grill. Cook for about 2–3 minutes per side. There should be defined grill marks. Serve with aioli and perhaps the Green Mango Salad (page 8).

Szechuan Ginger Stir Fry

Serves 4

A made-in-minutes (seven, to be exact) kaleidoscope stir-fry makes easy work of preparing a toothsome, accompanying side to whatever meaty-main that's been slow-cooking throughout the day.

1 tablespoon canola oil
2 tablespoons sesame oil
7 garlic cloves, minced
2 tablespoons fresh ginger, minced
3 large carrots, bias cut
2 stalks of celery, bias cut
1 small yellow onion, sliced
1 small red onion, sliced
2 whole zucchini, julienned
2 whole yellow squash, julienned
1 large red bell pepper, sliced lengthwise
2 tablespoons soy sauce
Kosher salt and coarse ground black pepper

In a large wok, add the oils and heat until there are visible ripples. Add the garlic and ginger and stir until fragrant, about 90 seconds. Working in batches, add the vegetables, each time ensuring that they get coated with the oil and aromatics. Sauté on high heat for 3 minutes, constantly stirring. Add the soy sauce around the rim of the wok and stir to ensure that the vegetables are slightly softened from the liquid and heat. Sauté for an additional 2 minutes then take off the heat. Season to taste and serve hot.

Garlicky Parmesan Shrimp & Fava Bean Ravioli with Spinach Almond Pesto

Serves 2–4

Trepidation is oftentimes the thief of attempts, when it comes to home-cooks making from-scratch, pasta-maker-pasta. That's why, this is the type of dish best made with the company of a friend and a bottle of Loire Valley, Sancerre. Time and elbow-grease go a long way in preparing this gorgeously rewarding dish bursting with the young crisp of spring.

1 cup fresh fava beans (about 1 pound young fava pods), peeled and shelled

1 cup good parmesan cheese, grated and divided

Salt and pepper to taste

2 tablespoons butter

5 cloves garlic, finely minced

¼ cup Vidalia onions, finely diced

1 pound shrimp (any size) peeled, deveined, and tails removed

½ teaspoon red pepper flakes

2 cups spinach

½ cup slivered almonds

Juice of 1 lemon

2 cups all-purpose flour

4 large eggs

⅓ cup extra-virgin olive oil

For the Favas: Shuck beans by opening the pod, simply by tearing off one end and "zipping" down the side, with the string-like membrane. After all the pods are removed, bring a large pot of salted water to a boil and add beans and cook until tender, 2–3 minutes. Transfer to an ice bath to stop the cooking. Drain and squeeze the beans with a clean kitchen cloth, add ¼ cup of the cheese and a pinch of salt, then pulse in a food processor until smooth. Transfer to a bowl and set aside.

For the Shrimp: In a sauté pan, on medium heat, melt the butter until it emits a nutty aroma. Add the garlic and onions and sauté until the onions are translucent and very fragrant. Add the shrimp and red pepper flakes, and cook for 5 minutes. Allow to cool, and chop the shrimp into very small pieces. Top with ¼ cup parmesan cheese and place in the bowl with fava beans. Refrigerate.

For the Pesto: In a food processor, pulse the spinach, almonds, remainder of the parmesan cheese, salt and pepper, and lemon juice. Slowly stream in the olive oil. Blend to combine.

For the Dough: On a large, clean work surface, mound the flour and create a well in the center. Crack the eggs into the well and very tenderly beat with a fork.

Gradually draw small amounts of flour from the outside of the mound into the inside, incorporating the eggs and still using a fork. Knead in all the flour until it is well incorporated into the eggs, for about 10 minutes, until the dough is smooth and elastic.

Divide the dough into quarters. Dust one quarter with flour, while keeping the other parts covered under a semi-damp clean kitchen cloth. Using a pasta maker, set the rollers to the widest setting and let the dough roll through for 3–5 iterations. Fold the dough and repeat the process, until the dough gets progressively narrower, adjusting the settings from wider to narrower. Continue this process until all the dough is used. There should be multiple sheets. *Cue the wine, as this entire process should take an hour.*

On a floured work surface, take one sheet of pasta dough and place a full tablespoon of the shrimp and fava bean filling on the dough. Space filling roughly three inches apart. Working with a pastry brush, wet with water and moisten the area of the dough that surrounds the filling. Take another sheet of pasta dough and place over the bottom half (containing the filling). Securely press around the mounds of filling to excrete any excess air and to tightly seal. Utilizing a pizza wheel, cut pasta into 2- or 3-inch squares (or using a cookie cutter, to achieve circular ravioli). At this point the raviolis could be frozen for future use. Then, in a large pot of salted, boiling water, add half the ravioli and give it one gentle stir. Allow to cook for 5–7 minutes then use a slotted spoon to transfer to a colander. Drain and keep warm. Repeat the process until all the ravioli is cooked.

During the interval, melt 4 tablespoons of butter in a skillet over medium-high heat. Allow the butter to cook until lightly browned. Add half the cooked ravioli to the butter and toss to coat. Remove with a slotted spoon and repeat the process. Add in the pesto to the finished raviolis and gingerly toss to coat. Transfer ravioli to a serving platter and sprinkle with freshly grated parmesan.

Shrimp Salade Nicoise
with Roasted Pineapple Vinaigrette

Serves 4–6

Wars of the culinary kind have been fought over the elements that comprise France's ubiquitous namesake salad. This variation dresses the classical components with a vinaigrette that's anything but classic.

FOR THE VINAIGRETTE
1 cup fresh pineapple, cubed
2 tablespoons honey
¼ cup rice vinegar
4 tablespoons extra-virgin olive oil
Salt and pepper to taste

FOR THE SALADE
1 pound new potatoes
Olive oil
Salt & pepper
4 large eggs, hard-boiled, peeled, and quartered
½ pound haricot verts, trimmed
1 pound shrimp (sized 16/20), cleaned and deveined
1 cup dry white wine, such as chardonnay
1 small onion, sliced
2 celery stalks, chopped
1 lemon, halved
2 sprigs fresh thyme
1 pint grape tomatoes
1 bunch watercress

Preheat oven to 350°F. Place the pineapple on a baking sheet and drizzle with half of the honey. Bake for 25–30 minutes until the firm texture of the pineapple has yielded and developed a slight char.

Remove the pan and allow the pineapple to cool. Then, combine in a blender or food processor along with the rest of the ingredients. Season to taste and set aside.

For the Potatoes: Place the potatoes in a medium saucepan; cover with cold water, and season the water generously with salt. On medium-high heat, allow the potatoes to simmer for about 7–10 minutes. Drain and transfer to a medium bowl. Drizzle with extra-virgin olive oil and sprinkle with salt and pepper. Set aside.

For the Haricot Verts: Refill the ice bath. In a pot (utilizing the same pot used for the preparing the potatoes is most efficient) with salted boiling water, add the haricot verts and allow them to cook for 2–4 minutes. Remove the haricot verts and promptly plunge into the ice bath for 1 minute. Remove from ice bath, drizzle with extra-virgin olive oil, and sprinkle with salt and pepper. Set aside.

For the Shrimp: To poach the shrimp, create a simple court bouillon by bringing two cups of water, the white wine, onion, celery, and thyme to a gentle simmer. Add the shrimp and allow to poach until firm and pink, about 3 minutes. Using a slotted spoon, remove shrimp from the poaching liquid and drizzle with extra-virgin olive oil and salt. Set aside.

To Assemble: Toss the watercress in the roasted pineapple vinaigrette. On a large platter, assemble the ingredients in a manner most appealing to you.

Shrimp, Ginger, and Scallion Lettuce Wraps

Serves 4

Your outdoor grill takes the backseat to this colorful play on traditional Vietnamese spring rolls. With simple-to-assemble components, these low-calorie powerhouse wraps have all the makings for a quick, warm-weather, build-your-own, al fresco dinner.

2 teaspoons sesame oil

1 pound (16/20) shrimp, peeled and deveined

½ teaspoon salt

½ teaspoon black pepper

2 teaspoons fresh ginger, minced

1 package rice or cellophane noodles

2 tablespoons rice vinegar

½ teaspoon red pepper flakes

2 tablespoons fresh lime juice

3 cloves garlic, minced

1 tablespoon brown sugar

¼ cup fish sauce

2 heads Boston or Butter lettuce (leaves separated from core, rinsed and pat dried)

1 large carrot, peeled and julienned

½ cup scallions, bias cut

⅓ cup wasabi peas or dry roasted peanuts, finely chopped as garnish

In a sauté pan over medium heat, add the sesame oil and sauté shrimp with salt, pepper, and half of the ginger until the shrimp is pink and firm, about 5 minutes. Transfer to a bowl and set aside.

In a large bowl with steaming hot water, add the rice noodles so they are completely submerged. Cover and set aside for 15 minutes. When the noodles are soft, drain the water and using kitchen shears, cut the noodles into thirds. Drizzle with a tad of rice vinegar, cover, and set aside.

In a small bowl, combine the chili flakes, lime juice, garlic, remaining ginger, brown sugar, and fish sauce. Whisk until the sugar is dissolved. Set aside.

To Assemble: Place the lettuce on a plate and add the rice noodles in the middle of the lettuce. This is followed by the shrimp, then the julienned carrots, scallions, and wasabi peas or peanuts for garnish. Drizzle with sauce.

Lobster Sunomono

Serves 2

The presence of jicama, carrots, and tarragon in this lobster salad makes this traditional Japanese cucumber and vinegar salad pulse with some of the West's beloved ingredients. It's undoubtedly an inventive main salad, that creates archetype in the flavor convergence of East meeting West.

½ cup rice vinegar
¼ cup mirin
½ teaspoon salt
1 teaspoon soy sauce
1 teaspoon gingerroot, grated
2 (1–1½ pound) lobsters
½ cup cucumber, shaved

½ cup jicama, shredded
½ cup carrots, shredded
¼ cup scallions, bias-cut
¼ cup fresh tarragon
Black sesame seeds to garnish,
    optional

For the Marinade: Whisk to combine the vinegar, mirin, salt, soy sauce, and ginger. Set aside.

For the Lobster: Plunge lobsters head first into a stock pot of heavily salted boiling water. Cover and let them cook atop a gentle boil for 12 minutes. Allow the lobsters to cool for 15 minutes. To remove the joints, twist the tail from the body, then twist and pull each of the claws. Repeat this same motion to separate the knuckle and claw. To remove the tail meat, allow the back of the tail shell to face upwards and with a chef's knife, cut the tail lengthwise in half. If there is roe present, it could be added to the succotash depending on preference. Scrape the meat from the shell and either leave the tail intact or cut into 1-inch pieces and set aside. When removing the knuckle and claw meat, crack the shell with the back of a chef's knife. With a bit of the meat exposed, gently wiggle the claw meat out of the shell. Set aside. To remove the knuckle meat, with a pair of kitchen shears cut along the smooth outer edge of the knuckle and using your fingers, pry the shell open and remove the meat. Discard the shells and reserve all the meat.

To Assemble: In a medium-sized bowl toss to combine the cucumbers, jicama, and carrots with the marinade. Very gently fold in the lobster meat, taking caution to keep the seafood intact. Season to taste. Add the aromatics, and garnish with black sesame seeds. Serve chilled.

Creole Bouillabaisse

Serves 4–6

This stew is an apt depiction of how you can replicate life on the islands, within your current locale. Creole Bouillabaisse differs from traditional French in that it does not employ the smokiness of saffron or the illusory hint of anise-flavored Pernod. In the French Caribbean, this one-pot dish also stays true to its storied origins; this Creole version was originally crafted by fishermen's wives from unsold portions from their husbands' daily catch. And although there are countless variations on this classic, this recipe stays simple and true to its original form.

4 tablespoons butter
¼ cup all-purpose flour
1 cup white onions, chopped
½ cup celery, chopped
2 garlic cloves, minced
¼ cup parsley, chopped
3 cups fish stock
2 (14-ounce) cans diced tomatoes
1 cup white wine
1 tablespoon fresh lemon juice
1 bay leaf
¼ teaspoon cayenne pepper
Salt and pepper to taste
1 pound fresh white fish, cubed
1 pound oyster meat, cut into bite-
    sized pieces
1 pound shrimp, peeled and deveined

In large pot or dutch oven, over medium heat, melt butter. Then prepare a roux by adding flour to the melted butter and consistently stirring until mixture is light brown. To the roux, add the onions, celery, garlic, and parsley, and continue stirring until vegetables are tender and fragrant. Gradually stir in fish stock. To this mixture add the remaining ingredients except the seafood.

Bring to a boil, and then simmer for 15 minutes. Following this, add the white fish and oysters and simmer for an additional 7 minutes. Add the shrimp and cook for 5 more minutes until it is cooked. Season to taste.

NOTE: If you do not already have fish stock on hand, make a batch by combining the shells of the shrimp with 2 carrots, 2 stalks of celery, and 1 large skin-on yellow onion (all rough chopped) as well as the stems from the parsley. Allow it to gently simmer for 30 minutes, in 1 quart of water, then strain.

Spring Pea & Ginger Risotto

Serves 4-6

The transience of Spring is all the magic. New life is pushing through the once frozen aridity of the earth, and with that comes a healthy crop of expectation and produce. This vegetarian risotto is an ode to the wonder of the season; marrying the creamy starch of rice to the fresh vitality of peas and the assertive snap of ginger. It's the best of spring, in one pot.

1 quart vegetable stock
1 tablespoon extra-virgin olive oil
1 tablespoon butter
1 medium-sized Vidalia onion, diced
2 cups Arborio rice
2½ cups dry white wine
2 tablespoons ginger, freshly grated
1½ cups spring peas, shelled
¾ cup parmesan cheese, freshly grated
Salt and pepper to taste

In a large stock pot, bring the vegetable stock to a low simmer.

In a rondeau pan or a wide, heavy-bottom sauté pan, melt the olive oil and the butter then add the onions. Sweat the onions on medium heat until they are very soft and translucent, but there shouldn't be any caramelization. Add the rice and stir until the grains are coated and they are mostly translucent, about 5 minutes. Pour in the wine and stir until all the wine has been completely absorbed into the rice. Next add the ginger and stir to incorporate. Then, pour some of the simmered stock, one ladle at a time, into the rice. Again, stir until the stock is completely absorbed. Continue this process until most of the stock has been incorporated into the rice. This should take roughly 20 minutes with continuous stirring. At this point, the rice should be creamy with a slight al-dente bite. Add the peas about 5–8 minutes prior to the rice being completely cooked. If needed, add a tad more stock. Fold in the parmesan cheese, season with salt and black pepper, and garnish with pea shoots.

Rum-Buttered "Rockaway" Jerk Wings

Serves 2–4

All the heat, energy, and positive vibes of Negril pulse throughout this batch of lip-licking, oven-baked wings. Coincidentally, these wings are best served alongside the tunes of Beres Hammond and a Red Stripe Lager.

3 tablespoons allspice berries (Pimento)
1 cup brown sugar, divided
7 cloves garlic
1 tablespoon ginger, freshly grated
1 Scotch bonnet pepper, seeded
1 tablespoon ground thyme
1 bunch green onions
2 teaspoons cinnamon
2 teaspoons nutmeg
1 tablespoon salt
1 tablespoon pepper
3 pounds chicken wings, joints split
2 cups dark rum
½ cup cola
¼ cup ketchup
3 tablespoons butter, cubed

Preheat oven to 350°F. In a food processor, or using a mortar and pestle, combine the allspice, ½ cup of brown sugar, garlic, ginger, Scotch bonnet pepper, thyme, green onion, cinnamon, nutmeg, salt, and pepper. Pat dry chicken wings and apply this rub all over the chicken, ensuring that all the wings are well coated. Place on a sheet pan and bake for 30–35 minutes until the chicken is cooked.

Meanwhile, make the glaze. In a small sauce pan, whisk to combine the rum, the other half of the brown sugar, cola, and ketchup. Bring this mixture to a boil, turn off heat, and slowly add in the butter. Brush this glaze all over the chicken. Place the wings back into the oven and utilizing the broil function, allow the glaze to adhere to the wings for 3 minutes.

Rosemary & Lemon Brick Chicken

Serves 4

Full disclosure: this recipe does not have any of the big-four ingredients. It is, however, my essential back-pocket chicken recipe and the one guests ask for by name when family and friends visit. I first sampled Brick Chicken during preparations for an 18-week apprenticeship in Italy at the Rome Sustainable Food Project. Prior to my travels I resolved to absorb as much as I could about the gastronomic heritage of the country—and practice my fledgling Italian—by spending time with Italian friends whose passion for sustainability mirrored my own. Little did I know that a simple chicken dinner at a small restaurant in Rhinebeck, New York, taught me more than any of the language books I was poring over at the time.

"Pollo al Mattone (Chicken under a Brick)—we have to get it!" my friend interjected as we deliberated over the menu. That evening, I understood the essence of Italian cooking. It was the masterful way peasants and country folk cooked what was in their gardens, rivers, and chicken coops. They prepared bountiful meals with equal parts economy and élan. And although every global culture can trace beloved recipes of yesteryear back to a time of necessity; this brick chicken blunts every stereotype that frugal cooking is in any way cheap. In my opinion, it's the very opposite.

The wonder in this dish is that the weight of the brick presses into the meat, slightly breaking the bones and allowing the bird to be both succulent and crispy at the same time. I sear the bird in a large rondeau pan (or any wide, shallow pot) and finish in the oven at 350°F.

2 bricks, wrapped in a layer of aluminum foil
2 tablespoons kosher salt
1 tablespoon coarse ground black pepper
2 teaspoons cumin
1 tablespoon fresh rosemary, chopped
1 tablespoon fresh thyme, chopped

2 tablespoons garlic, minced
2 tablespoons extra-virgin olive oil
1 whole (3-pound) fryer chicken, rinsed and pat dried
Zest of 2 large lemons (cut the lemons in half after zesting)
1 large lemon, quartered, for garnish
1 spring rosemary, for garnish

In a small bowl, combine the spices, lemon zest, and aromatics. Set aside. Place oil in the pan and heat over medium. Do not allow the oil to reach smoking temperature. On a cutting board large enough to accommodate the bird, using kitchen shears or a sharp chef's knife, turn the poultry breast side down and cut through the backbone (or remove completely). This process of splitting and flattening a chicken is called spatchcocking. Rinse and pat dry the cavity. Using the spice mixture, generously season the cavity and the outer parts of the fryer.

Preheat oven to 350°F.

Place the bird in the pan skin side down, and place foil-wrapped bricks on top of the bird. Allow the bird to develop a golden brown sear and cook for about 20 minutes. After 20 minutes, remove the bricks and using tongs, gently turn the bird over so the seared breast side is facing upwards. Place the bricks on top of the bird, and place in oven. Cook for 35–40 minutes. Garnish with lemon quarters and rosemary.

Bacon, Shrimp, and Jalapeño Bloody Mary

Serves 2

When constructing a Bloody Mary, there are certain must-haves that need be met: the pucker of tomato juice, the heat of horseradish, the zing of fresh lemon, the meaty heft of Worcestershire, and the kick of the vodka. After that, all other accoutrements are up to your imagination.

4 ounces (half a cup) premium vodka

4 dashes Worcestershire sauce

2 dashes Tabasco

1 teaspoon prepared horseradish

2 tablespoons fresh lemon juice

1½ cups tomato juice

1 lemon, quartered

2 stalks celery, cut in half, including the leafy tops

2 slices bacon, cooked

2 pieces shrimp, steamed, tail-on

2 jalapeños

In a tumbler or beer glass filled with ice cubes, combine the vodka, Worcestershire sauce, tabasco, horseradish, lemon juice, and tomato juice. Cover with another tumbler of equal shape and size and "roll" the contents from one glass to another a few times. Following this, ensure that each tumbler has equal amounts of ice and the cocktail. Garnish with lemon and celery stalks, then skewer the bacon, shrimp, and jalapeño. Serve immediately.

Knight & Bishop

Serves 4

You get a noble cocktail, befitting its name when you douse a demerara sugar cube in Angostura Bitters, then muddle it with orange zest, drown it in Canton, and top it with the busty effervescence of hard ginger beer.

4 Demerara sugar cubes
Angostura bitters (5–6 dashes per sugar cube)
Zest of 1 large orange
4 ounces Domaine de Canton
1 (12-ounce) bottle of Crabbies ginger beer

In a chilled rocks glass, add the sugar cube and dash with bitters. Using a cocktail muddler, macerate the cube in the bitters. Add the orange zest, then the Canton. Top with ginger beer. Prepare for seconds.

Old School Bananas Foster

Serves 4

Immortalized by delight alone, this 1950s recipe hailing from the storied Brennan's Restaurant in the French Quarter of New Orleans, needs little introduction or alteration. It truly is perfect in its composition and ability to wow decade after decade.

4 tablespoons unsalted butter, cubed
½ cup brown sugar
½ teaspoon cinnamon
3 not-quite-ripe bananas, halved
   lengthwise, then bias cut
½ cup dark rum
1 pint good vanilla ice cream

In a heavy skillet or cast iron pan, on medium-low heat, melt the butter then add the brown sugar and cinnamon. Stir until the sugar dissolves. Add the bananas and cook for about 1–1½ minutes per side. As the bananas are cooking, using a long-handled spoon, spoon the sauce over the bananas. Remove the skillet from the heat, then carefully add the rum. Using a lighter or long match, ignite the bananas mixture, again basting the bananas with the sauce until the flame naturally extinguishes.

Divide the ice cream into 4 bowls, top each with bananas and sauce. Serve immediately.

Coconut Layer Cake

Serves 6–8

This deceptively straightforward darling confection of the American South will make a master-baker out of many reluctant home cooks. The use of some ingenious tricks camouflages any faux-pas, producing a cake that looks (almost) as good as it tastes.

FOR THE CAKE

1½ cups (3 sticks) unsalted butter, room temperature
2⅔ cups sugar
5 eggs, room temperature
Rind of a small orange
1½ teaspoons vanilla extract
1½ teaspoons almond extract
2⅓ cups cake flour
4 teaspoons baking powder
½ teaspoon baking soda
1 teaspoon salt
1½ cups full-fat, unsweetened coconut milk

FOR THE ICING

1 pound cream cheese, room temperature
2 sticks unsalted butter, room temperature
¼ cup coconut milk
1 teaspoon vanilla extract
1 pound confectioners' sugar, sifted
4 ounces shredded coconut
4 ounces toasted coconut flakes

Prepare the Cake: Preheat oven to 350°F. Outfit your cake pans first with a generous spread of butter, following with parchment paper then butter again, and finishing with slight dusting of flour. In an electric mixer fitted with the paddle attachment, cream together the butter and sugar for 5–7 minutes on high speed until it is airy and pale yellow. Following this, lower the speed to a slow-medium and add the room temperature eggs one at a time. Then add the orange rind. The mixture will look a bit curdled.

Fret not. Add the vanilla and almond extracts. In a separate bowl combine the cake flour, baking powder, baking soda, and salt. Ready your coconut milk. Working in batches, add the flour to the mixing bowl, then a bit of the coconut milk. Continue this alternating process, always starting and ending with the flour mixture and scraping the bowl in between with a rubber spatula. Mix for another 2–3 minutes. Remove the rind. Pour into prepared cake pans and bake for 35 minutes. Gingerly remove from cake pans and allow to cool on a wire rack.

For the Icing: In the bowl of an electric mixer fitted with the paddle attachment, combine the cream cheese, butter, coconut milk, and vanilla extract on low speed. Add the confectioners' sugar and mix until very smooth.

To Assemble: On a cake stand, take one layer, top side down and smear with icing. Place the second layer atop, and frost the top and sides as evenly and smoothly as possible. Lightly press shredded coconut onto the sides of the cake and decorate the top with the toasted coconut flakes. Serve room temperature with a glass of for-no-reason-at-all champagne.

SUMMER

Late Nights & Endless Libations

Light Fare

Stacked Tomato Salad with Balsamic Glazed Shrimp / 32

White Coconut Gazpacho / 34

Coconut Panzanella Salad / 35

Corn on the Cob with Basil Butter & Coconut Salt / 37

Mojito Marinated Veggie Kabobs / 38

Toasted Coconut West Indies Crab Salad / 41

Mains

Coconut & Sweet Corn Chowder / 42

Summer Squash Pad Thai / 44

Avocado Coconut Cream Soup / 45

Soft-Shell Crab Sandwich with Bi-Color Slaw & Lemon Ginger Tartar Sauce / 46

The Lobster Roll / 48

Lobster Summer Succotash / 49

To Sip

Grapefruit Ginger Prosecco Popsicles / 50

Barthelemy 75 / 52

Tall, Dark, and Stormy / 55

Blueberry Mint Coconut Cooler / 55

Rum on the Rocks / 56

Sweet Endings

Grilled Strawberry & Ginger Shortcake / 57

Coconut, Mango, and Mint Granita / 58

Grilled Stone Fruit Drizzled with Piña Colada Fondue / 59

Stacked Tomato Salad with Balsamic Glazed Shrimp

Serves 3

Effortless elegance need not be an oxymoron. In fact, this 10-minute summer staple parlays the two seeming dualities into a dinner party worthy preparation. For even greater visual interest, incorporate different types of gargantuan summer tomatoes, wait, then listen to the crescendo of applause from your doting diners.

3 large ripe tomatoes (1 for each guest)
Flaky sea salt, such as Maldon
Coarse ground black pepper
½ cup balsamic vinegar
1 tablespoon brown sugar
9 pieces shrimp
3 large cloves garlic, finely minced

1 tablespoon butter
3 large basil leaves (smash between hands)
3 (¼-inch) slices fresh mozzarella cheese
¼ cup basil, chiffonade

Using a serrated knife, cut off the very top and very bottom of the tomatoes so that the tomato sits perfectly flat on the plate. Then slice the tomato in half lengthwise. Season each half with salt and pepper. Set aside.

Make the Glaze: Over medium heat, combine the balsamic vinegar, sugar, and a pinch of salt into a saucepan. Once the vinegar is boiling, give it a quick stir and allow it to cook until it reduces by half. Allow it to cool and set aside.

Make the Shrimp: Pat dry the shrimp and add the salt, pepper, and garlic. In a sauté pan, add the butter and allow it to melt until brown, nutty, and fragrant. Add the shrimp and sauté for 3 minutes per side. Remove from heat and set aside.

Construct the Plate: Place a small dab of the balsamic glaze in the middle of the plate and rest the bottom half of a tomato directly on the glaze. Then place the basil across the tomato so that the pointed end is visible. Follow with the mozzarella cheese and cap with the top of the tomato inverted, so that the fleshy interior is exposed. Position the shrimp on top of the tomato, in an interlocking manner so that each piece is tethered to the other. Drizzle the glaze on top of the shrimp and garnish with the chiffonade of basil.

SUMMER

White Coconut Gazpacho

Serves 4

From humble beginnings from the Andalucian region in Spain, this once misconceived chunky, tomato-based cold soup gets a clean, smooth, refined facelift.

4 slices crustless sourdough bread

6 tablespoons coconut oil, divided

4 cups cold coconut water

3 cups cucumber, peeled and small-diced

1½ cups honeydew melon, cubed

1 cup green grapes, divided

1 cup slivered almonds, slightly toasted

2 cloves garlic, minced

1 cup plain whole-milk Greek yogurt

1 tablespoon white wine vinegar

Juice of ½ a lime

2 teaspoons honey

Kosher salt for garnish

2 tablespoons fresh chives, finely chopped

2 tablespoons slivered almonds, toasted

Make Croutons: Preheat oven to 350°F. Cut two slices of the sourdough into a small dice. In a bowl toss the bread cubes with half the coconut oil (reserve the rest for garnish) and two pinches of salt, then spread on a baking sheet. The cubes should bake until crisp, for 8–10 minutes.

For the Gazpacho: Take the remainder of the bread and soak it the coconut water for a 2–3 minutes, until it is saturated. Blend the soaked bread (with the coconut water), cucumber, melon, half the grapes, almonds, garlic, and yogurt. Strain through a sieve, pressing down heavily to extract the liquid ingredients, into a bowl. Following this, briskly whisk in 1 tablespoon of the coconut oil, white wine vinegar, lime juice, and honey until very smooth. Season to taste with salt and chill until cold. Garnish with the remainder of the grapes, croutons, chives, slivered almonds, and a drizzle of coconut oil.

Coconut Panzanella Salad

Serves 4

Panzanella is one of those recipes that shouldn't actually be considered a recipe. This dish is a testament of the genius of cucina povera *and the masterful way Tuscans of yesteryear made joyous use of the ingredients on hand, even if said ingredients were stale, or less than stellar. This panzanella pays tribute to the spirit of purpose and invention. In this adaptation, the stale baguette is lightly tossed and toasted in coconut oil and dense, over-ripe tomatoes are given a second chance to shine.*

1 day-old baguette, cut into cubes
¼ cup coconut oil, liquefied
Salt and pepper to taste
¼ cup extra-virgin olive oil
2 tablespoons red wine vinegar
2 cloves garlic, smashed and minced
Half a small red onion, thinly sliced
2 pounds over-ripe tomatoes, cut into wedges
2 cups cucumber, cubed
1 cup hand-torn basil
Shaved pecorino Romano, optional for topping

Preheat oven to 400°F. On a sheet pan, toss the bread in the coconut oil and lightly season with salt and pepper. Toast for 7–10 minutes until the bread is golden brown and has a little crunch. The bread should not be as crunchy as croutons.

In a large bowl, whisk to combine the olive oil, red wine vinegar, and garlic. To this, add the red onions, tomatoes, and cucumbers. Toss well to combine and season to taste with salt and black pepper. Add the bread and finally the hand-torn basil. Allow to salad to sit for 20–30 minutes prior to serving.

Corn on the Cob with Basil Butter & Coconut Salt

Serves 4

Sweet corn is probably one of summer's greatest equalizers—quick, cheap, and deliriously addictive. It's always best to shuck and serve a few extra ears because appetites run high for this seasonal gem, especially when robed in basil butter and sprinkled with home-made finishing salt.

FOR THE BASIL BUTTER
½ cup (1 stick) unsalted butter, room temperature
¼ cup fresh basil, finely chopped
1 teaspoon freshly squeezed lemon juice
Salt & pepper to taste

COCONUT SALT
2 tablespoons unsweetened coconut flakes
2 tablespoons good sea salt, like Fleur de Sel
4 ears freshly shucked sweet summer corn

Prepare the Butter: In a small bowl or in an electric mixer fitted with the paddle attachment, combine all the ingredients and mix until well combined.

Using a rubber spatula, transfer to a large piece of parchment paper. Roll into a cylinder about 4 inches long with a 1-inch diameter. Twist the ends of paper to seal, and refrigerate for 90 minutes or until very firm. Cut crosswise to serve.

For the Corn: In a mortar & pestle, gently combine the salt and coconut flakes. Bring a large stock pot of salted water to a rolling boil. Add the corn and cover the pot and turn off the heat. Allow the corn to cook in the hot water for about 5–7 minutes, depending on the size of the corn. Using tongs, remove the corn; drench with basil butter and sprinkle with coconut salt.

Mojito Marinated Veggie Kabobs

Serves 4

This upbeat skewered side incorporates the musings of that classic Cuban cocktail—rum, lime, and hand-torn mint—and allows for the most unassuming of vegetables to shine under the spotlight of utility.

3 tablespoons brown sugar

1 shallot, peeled and very finely diced

¼ cup extra-virgin olive oil

½ cup dark rum

½ cup lime juice (about 3 limes)

Zest of 1 lime

¾ cup fresh mint, divided—½ cup chopped and the other ¼ cup hand torn

8 large button mushrooms, sliced thick

1 medium red onion, cut in chunks

1 medium yellow squash, sliced thick

1 medium zucchini, sliced thick

1 large red bell pepper, cored, seeded, cut into chunks

1 large yellow bell pepper, cored, seeded, cut into chunks

1 large green bell pepper, cored, seeded, cut into chunks

1 pint cherry tomatoes

In a large bowl, whisk to combine the brown sugar, shallots, olive oil, rum, lime juice, lime zest, and chopped mint. Add the chopped vegetables to the marinade and using your hands, make sure each piece is coated by the marinade.

Skewer the vegetables in any manner most appealing to you. Place on a hot outdoor grill or stove-top grill pan, and grill for 2–3 minutes per side. Garnish with the hand-torn mint.

NOTE: If employing wooden skewers, soak them in water for 1 minute, this will prevent them from burning on an open fire grill.

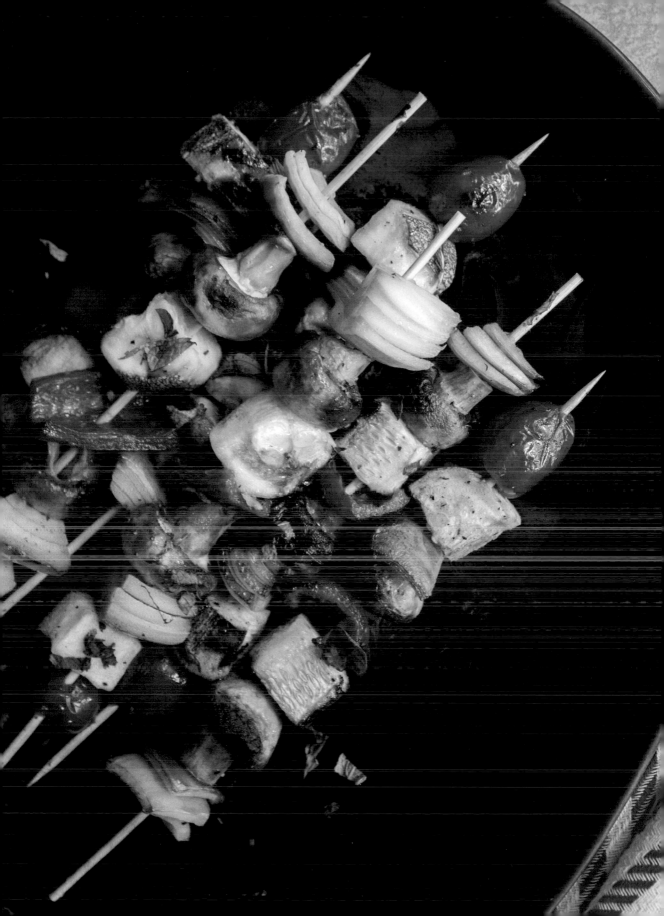

Toasted Coconut West Indies Crab Salad

Serves 4-6

A low-country tradition hailing from South Alabama is translated into a crunchy canape by the inclusion of coconut and a spicy fried wonton.

1 teaspoon salt
1 teaspoon pepper
½ teaspoon cayenne pepper
Zest of ½ lime
4–6 cups vegetable oil
10 square wonton wrappers, sliced diagonally to make 20 triangles
Juice from 1 lemon
¼ cup apple cider vinegar
½ cup olive oil
1 pound lump crab meat
½ cup Vidalia onions, thinly sliced
¼ cup unsweetened coconut flakes, toasted

For the Wontons: In a small bowl, stir to combine the salt, pepper, cayenne, and lime zest. Set aside.

Ready a paper towel–lined plate.

Pour the vegetable oil into a heavy bottom pot, over medium high heat, for 3 minutes, until the oil is hot. Gently place each triangle into the oil, and fry, turning once, for 15–20 seconds per side. Do not crowd the pot—fry 3 or 4 wontons at a time. Using a slotted spoon, remove the fried wontons, place onto paper towel–lined plate and immediately season both sides of the wonton with the seasoning mix.

For the Crab Salad: In a medium-sized bowl, whisk to combine the lemon juice, apple cider vinegar, and olive oil. Add the crab meat and Vidalia onions and gently toss to combine. Add salt and pepper to taste, and top with toasted coconut. Place atop seasoned wonton.

Coconut & Sweet Corn Chowder

Serves 4

It's easy to eat a predominantly raw diet over the summer. There's a seemingly endless crop of vegetables that snap of just-picked freshness, as well as peaches, berries, and plums that drip with a nectar only sun-ripeness could produce. However, there are the days that are anomalies, when you long for something not only cooked, but hearty and comforting. And for those days, there is this soup.

1 tablespoon coconut oil
3 slices thick-cut bacon, chopped
1 large (about 2 cups) sweet Vidalia onion, medium diced
2 large carrots, medium diced
2 stalks celery, medium diced
1 red bell pepper, small dice
4 medium Yukon Gold potatoes, small dice

3 cups chicken stock
2 cups coconut water
1 tablespoon fresh thyme, chopped
3 cups fresh corn kernels (save the cob)
1 (14-ounce) can coconut milk
Salt and black pepper to taste
Plum tomatoes & fresh basil to garnish

In a heavy bottom stock pan on medium heat, melt the coconut oil until fragrant. Add the bacon and cook until crisp and golden brown. Remove the bacon with a slotted spoon, place on paper towel, and set aside. To the coconut oil and bacon pan drippings, add the onions, carrots, celery, bell pepper, and a generous pinch of salt, and cook for about 10 minutes or until the vegetables are tender. Next add the potatoes, chicken stock, coconut water, and fresh thyme. Allow the chowder to cook for 15–20 minutes. Add the kernels along with the cobs to the chowder, and cook for 5–7 minutes. Using tongs, remove the cobs and discard. Reduce heat to low and gradually stir in the coconut milk. Cook for another 3 minutes and season to taste with salt and coarse ground pepper and remove from heat.

For the Garnish: In a small bowl, combine the tomatoes, bacon, and basil with a pinch of salt and pepper. Toss to combine and serve atop chowder.

Summer Squash Pad Thai

Serves 2-4

You'll have a hard time remembering that this summertime spin on Thai's most lauded dish was made with anything but fresh ribboned zucchini and bright seasonal yellow squash.

Juice of 3 limes
1 tablespoon hoisin sauce
¼ cup coconut milk
1 tablespoon soy sauce or tamari
½ tablespoon red pepper flakes
2 teaspoons mirin
½ tablespoon kosher salt
½ tablespoon coarse ground black
    pepper
¼ cup roasted salted peanuts or
    cashews
½ tablespoon coconut oil

2 cloves garlic, minced
1 tablespoon fresh ginger, grated
1 medium Vidalia onion, thinly sliced
1 large yellow summer squash,
    julienned
1 large zucchini, julienned
5–7 sprigs cilantro + 1 tablespoon,
    roughly chopped
5 sprigs green onion, bias cut through
    greens and whites
2 limes, quartered

Make the sauce for the pad Thai by combining in a large bowl, the lime juice, hoisin sauce, coconut milk, soy sauce, chili flakes, mirin, salt, and pepper until well combined. Set aside.

Chop the nuts, or using a food processor, pulse until nuts are no longer whole, but definitely not ground into a powder. Set aside.

In a wok or large skillet over medium-high heat, add the oil, garlic, ginger, and onions. Sauté until onions are tender but not overly soft and the aromatics are fragrant. Add the zucchini, squash, and cilantro and stir to combine about 2 minutes. Stir in the reserved sauce and nuts. Garnish with cilantro, green onions, and lime wedges.

Avocado Coconut Cream Soup

Serves 4-6

The subtlety of this refreshing yet filling soup is only outdone by the ease of preparation. A close kin to vichyssoise, the garlic and coconut add a hint of complexity without placing too much demand on avocado.

3 large ripe avocados, peeled and chopped
2 cloves garlic
1 cup coconut milk
2 cups vegetable stock
½ teaspoon lime juice
½ teaspoon hot pepper sauce
1 teaspoon cilantro, finely chopped
Coarse salt and ground black pepper

Place the chopped avocados and garlic in a blender or food processor and puree until smooth. Add the coconut milk and blend, on high. In a large bowl, combine the vegetable stock with the avocado puree and stir vigorously until all the ingredients are evenly incorporated. In a fine-mesh sieve, pass the mixture through then stir in the lime juice, hot sauce, and cilantro. Season to taste with salt and black pepper and refrigerate for at least two hours prior to serving.

Soft-Shell Crab Sandwich with Bi-Color Slaw & Lemon Ginger Tartar Sauce

Serves 4

The sweet tasting blue crab is the most widely employed crab in the United States. In the Caribbean, however, there are myriad species of crab and even more ways to prepare them. This show-stopper of a sandwich uses blue crab which are in a transitional stage, in that they have recently molted their old exoskeleton in preparation for a new one. They are therefore still soft and wholly edible, save for the mouthparts, gills, and abdomen. The culinary clamor for soft-shells is real and worth every bit of hype, because once those crabs shed that old shell, a replacement shell begins forming and hardening within hours. There's only a narrow window when the tenacity of fishermen yields the tastiest of results, in this instance a lightly breaded crab, topped with slaw, and anchored by an unexpected tartar sauce.

FOR THE SLAW
1 tablespoon champagne vinegar
½ cup mayonnaise
1 teaspoon celery seeds
2 teaspoons sugar
1 cup purple cabbage, thinly sliced
1 cup white cabbage, thinly sliced
Kosher salt and freshly ground
    pepper

FOR THE TARTAR SAUCE
½ cup very good mayo
1 tablespoon dill relish
Juice of 1 lemon
2 tablespoons ginger, freshly grated
Salt and pepper to taste

FOR THE CRAB
2–2½ cups vegetable oil
½ cup all-purpose flour
2 tablespoons Old Bay seasoning
Kosher salt and freshly ground pepper
2 eggs
½ teaspoon chili flakes
1 cup panko breadcrumbs
4 soft-shell crabs, cleaned
4 large knot-rolls, warmed

For the Slaw: In a bowl, combine vinegar, mayonnaise, celery seeds, and sugar. Add the cabbage and evenly coat. Season to taste with salt and pepper. Chill in refrigerator.

NOTE: If uncleaned, prepare the soft-shells by washing them and cutting off the face just behind the eyes. Gently lift the top of the shell and remove the spongy fingers and/or the black apron. Female crabs tend to have characteristic stripe markings. Rinse the crab in cold water and dry.

For the Tartar Sauce: In a bowl, whisk together all of the ingredients. Season to taste with salt and pepper. Chill in refrigerator.

For the Crab: In a large skillet, over medium-high heat, place vegetable oil and allow it to heat.

Using 3 large shallow bowls, construct a standard breading station. In the first bowl combine the flour with Old Bay, salt, and pepper. In the second bowl, create an egg wash by beating both eggs together. And in the third bowl, add the breadcrumbs and season with Old Bay, salt, pepper, and chili flakes.

When working with seafood, it is imperative to always have a clean and dry (plastic) cutting board as well as a clean and dry fish, or in this case, crustacean.

Dredge the crab in the flour, shaking off excess. Next, dip the flour-coated crab in the egg-wash and drip off the excess. Following this, evenly coat the crab in the breadcrumbs and promptly place, shell side down, into the hot oil. Fry for about 3–4 minutes per side, until the crabs are golden brown. Repeat the process for all 4 crabs and immediately sprinkle with kosher salt when they are cooked.

Assemble by spreading the tartar sauce on the bun, then the fried soft-shell, capping it with slaw, and then another spread of tartar sauce on the top of the bun. Serve with a beastly cold lager and devour.

The Lobster Roll

Serves 4

Lobster meat baptized in coconut compound butter. A toasted top split bun. A squirt of lemon juice. A smear of Old Bay aioli. Celery leaf garnish. 'Nuf said.

FOR THE COCONUT COMPOUND BUTTER
⅓ cup coconut oil, solid
Zest of 1 lemon
½ teaspoon red pepper flakes
1 teaspoon salt

FOR THE ROLL
2 tablespoons + 2 teaspoons lemon
    juice
¼ cup full-fat mayonnaise
3 teaspoons Old Bay
4 (1½-pound) live lobsters
½ stick butter, melted
4 top-split hot dog buns
¼ cup celery leaves, roughly chopped
Salt to taste

In a small bowl, mash together the solid coconut oil with the lemon zest, red pepper flakes, and salt, until evenly combined. Spoon this mixture onto a sheet of parchment paper and shape into a log. Secure the ends of the log by twisting and refrigerate until ready to use.

Briskly whisk 1 teaspoon of lemon juice, mayonnaise, and Old Bay seasoning. Add a pinch of salt and set aside.

Prepare the live lobsters, as outlined in directions on page 17.

Toss the lobster meat with the remaining lemon juice, salt, and half of the melted compound butter.

Heat a grill pan or stove-top griddle and brush the entire bun with melted butter, both the outside and the inside of the bun. Toast the bun until slightly golden. Smear the aioli on the inside of the bun. Divide the lobster among the buns. Sprinkle with celery leaves.

Lobster Summer Succotash

Serves 2-4

With a riot of color, this dish defines summer eating. The sweet Vidalias are sweated in olive oil and with the clean heft of smashed garlic, this unassuming blend of aromatics produces a base of flavor, one that is nothing short of culinary nobility—it's probably why it's been used for centuries. A generous sprinkle of kosher salt draws out more mineral-laced jus from the garlic and onions, to which firm zucchini and yellow squash, crisp sweet corn, and soy-rich edamame are added. The smell alone trumps every other sensory experience. The tomatoes add vivid hue, and the final addition of basil and lemon makes for an exquisitely simple dish.

And then there's the lobster. What I love most about the king of the crustaceans, is that there's no need to wrestle with it to exact the end result you want. Extracting the dense buttery flesh does require a lesson in patience, but it is worth it. As Michael Polan noted, "It is common knowledge the first intrepid lobster eater was on to something very good." This seafood is brilliant in its reliability—with just a classic poach it steals the show, every time.

FOR THE LOBSTERS
2 (1-pound) Maine lobsters

Prepare and handle the lobster meat according to the instructions on page 17. Set aside.

FOR THE SUCCOTASH
2 tablespoons good olive oil
½ cup Vidalia onions, chopped
3 cloves garlic, smashed
¼ cup coconut milk

1 cup zucchini, diced
1 cup summer squash, diced
½ cup frozen shelled edamame, thawed
1 cup corn kernels (from 2 ears of corn)
½ cup tomatoes, diced, or equivalent amount of cherry tomatoes, halved
3 tablespoons basil, chopped
Juice of 1 large lemon
Kosher salt and coarse black pepper, to taste

In a sauté pan over medium high heat, add the olive oil and heat until slightly fragrant. Add the onions and a generous pinch of kosher salt—the salt will exact some of the sweet juices from the onions. Stir until the onions have softened. Add the garlic and allow to cook for another minute. Add the coconut milk and remaining vegetables, save for the basil, and sauté until the tomatoes lose their shape, about 5 minutes. Turn off the heat and stir in the lobster, basil, lemon juice, and season to taste.

Grapefruit Ginger Prosecco Popsicles

Serves 6-8

Long before parties were hashtagged, event extraordinaire Elsa Maxwell wrote in her 1957 book (and my still-relevant personal party manifesto) How to Do It: or The Lively Art of Entertaining, *"The best you can offer your guests is the unexpected." Here summer's most ubiquitous frozen treat gets an unexpected pop by being plunged in a flute full of prosecco. And while variations abound for this ingenious take on a mimosa, a little elbow grease and simplicity goes a long way. A store-bought popsicle, for instance, is oftentimes overly syrupy, and when it (inevitably) melts, that sticky residual juice is a quick way to ruin a good glass of bubbly. When curating that esoteric outdoor soiree, opt for two-ingredient, homemade popsicles, utilizing ingredients that naturally play on the contours of sparkling wine, such as citrus. Here hand-squeezed grapefruit juice and ginger serve up the simple with the famously unexpected.*

2 cups freshly squeezed grapefruit juice
½ cup roughly chopped ginger
1 cup sugar
1 cup water
1 bottle Prosecco, chilled

Ginger Simple Syrup: In a saucepan over medium-high heat, combine the ginger, sugar, and water. Allow to boil for 10 minutes until viscous. Remove from heat and allow it to cool completely.

In a small pitcher or spouted glass, combine the grapefruit juice and ¼ cup of the ginger simple syrup. Pour into popsicle molds and freeze as per manufacturer's instructions.

To Serve: Pour prosecco into chilled flutes. Very tenderly, remove the popsicles from the molds and immediately place into flutes. With glass in hand, promptly pose for a picture.

Barthelemy 75

Serves 4

This is a Caribbeanized take on the world's most beloved champagne cocktail, The French 75. Here, some of the West Indies' most ubiquitous ingredients are inverted to create a cocktail that stealthily tempers the potency of the strong spirit, while simultaneously embracing the crisp, forgiving rush of champagne.

1 cup brown sugar
4 ounces dark rum
Juice of 2 limes
4 ounces passion fruit juice
Dash of Angostura bitters
1 bottle champagne, chilled

Bring 1 cup of water and 1 cup brown sugar to a boil. Allow to cool completely.

In a cocktail shaker filled ¼ of the way with ice, combine the rum, lime juice, passion fruit juice, ¼ cup brown sugar simple syrup, and bitters. Shake until chilled.

Strain just shy of ¾ of the way into four champagne flutes, then top with champagne.

Make another batch.

Tall, Dark, and Stormy

Serves 4

Barring the name, there's absolutely nothing ominous in this colonial cocktail hailing from Bermuda's English Navy days. In this version, spiked ginger beer and Domaine de Canton liqueur makes this drink stand a bit taller from its original intent.

1 cup dark rum
1 (12-ounce) bottle Crabbie's ginger beer
1 lime, quartered
½ cup Domaine de Canton (ginger liqueur)

In a highball glass, filled a quarter of the way with ice, pour the rum, then the ginger liqueur. Squeeze the juice of 1 lime quarter into each glass, leaving the lime also in the glass. Top with ginger beer.

Blueberry Mint Coconut Cooler

Serves 1

Blueberries are antioxidant powerhouses, and mint is the unsung hero of herbs, with its capacity for boosting memory and mental dexterity. Here, a few simple, seasonal, farm-box finds up the ante on nature's electrolyte-rich wonder water.

¼ cup blueberries
5 mint leaves
1 pint coconut water, chilled

Gently muddle blueberries and mint in a mortar and pestle and top with coconut water.

Rum on the Rocks

Serves any and all

Premium Caribbean rum shines with versatility. Each bottle boasts distinct range, intrigue, and layers of flavors coming from the derivative sweetness of tropical fruits as well as the demur char of the oak vats in which they are aged. By incorporating only two ingredients and a silicon ice mold, this cocktail galvanizes rum's position as an exciting and inexpensive spirit, worthy to sip without much intervention.

Coconut water
Dark rum, as desired

Using a large silicone ice mold, freeze coconut water per manufacturer's instructions. Once frozen, remove from mold, place into a glass, and pour rum over the ice.

Grilled Strawberry & Ginger Shortcake

Serves 4

This dessert, an icon of Americana, takes an impressive and unexpected turn when the berries of high-summer are slathered in a honey-ginger dressing, charred on an open fire, then sandwiched between two pillowy biscuits.

1½ cups all-purpose flour
2 tablespoons sugar
½ teaspoon salt
¼ teaspoon baking soda
2 teaspoons baking powder
1 stick butter, chilled and cubed
2 cups cold heavy cream, divided

1 tablespoon + 1 teaspoon fresh
   ginger, grated
1 tablespoon lemon juice
2 tablespoons honey
1 pound fresh strawberries, left whole,
   tops removed
2 tablespoons confectioners' sugar
½ teaspoon vanilla extract

Prepare the Cakes: Preheat oven to 425°F. In a large mixing bowl, sift together the dry ingredients (flour, sugar, salt, baking soda, and baking powder). Using a pastry cutter, add the chilled butter to the mixture and combine until the butter is small yet still visible within the flour—it should now resemble coarse meal. Stream in 1 cup of the heavy cream. On a lightly floured surface, knead the dough for about 90 seconds, then using your hands, gently shape dough into an oval-rectangle and pat dough to a rough ½-inch thickness. Using a biscuit cutter, cut an even number of rounds, since you will need 2 per serving.

Place the biscuit rounds on a greased baking sheet, and bake for 12–14 minutes until golden brown. Remove from oven, and if desired, lightly brush with a little butter. Set aside.

Preheat grill. In a small bowl, combine the ginger, lemon juice, and honey. Skewer the strawberries (about 3–4 to a skewer depending on size), brush them with the ginger mixture and grill for 2–3 minutes per side until char-marks develop. Remove from grill, brush again with ginger mixture, and set aside on a plate. Continue this process until all the strawberries have been utilized. Do not discard the ginger mixture.

For the Chantilly Cream: In the bowl of an electric mixer fitted with the whisk attachment, combine the rest of the heavy cream, confectioners' sugar, and vanilla. Whisk until firm peaks develop, being careful not to overmix.

To Assemble: Place 1 biscuit on a plate and lightly brush the top side of the biscuit with the honey-ginger mixture. Next, place 3–4 pieces of the whole, grilled strawberries on top of the biscuit. Add a dollop of Chantilly cream, then cap with another biscuit. If desired, top off with more Chantilly cream. Devour.

Coconut, Mango, and Mint Granita

Serves 4

Fresh mangoes insist on the right to add brilliant hue to what would potentially be a delicious, yet monochromatic intermezzo. This made-in-10-minutes, semi-frozen dinner party staple is a fitting way to transition between courses or to book-end a meal. The coconut adds dimension and subtle sweetness, and the cooling linear notes of the mint ensures that this coarse sorbet is above all else, very well balanced.

1 large ripe mango
⅓ cup fresh mint, chopped
2 cups coconut water
2 teaspoons fresh lemon juice
2 tablespoons granulated sugar

Using a paring knife, peel the skin off the mango. Remove the flesh, extracting as much as possible from around the pit. Place the mango in a blender along with the mint, coconut water, lemon juice, and sugar. Blend the ingredients until well combined, about 2–3 minutes. Pour the mixture into a rectangular dish and place into the freezer. Every 20 minutes, remove the bowl and using a fork, agitate the freezing process by scraping the ice crystals, so that it yields a fluffy, icy consistency.

SUMMER

Grilled Stone Fruit Drizzled with Piña Colada Fondue

Serves 4-6

The once-ubiquitous summer staples—peach cobbler and the piña colada—get a modern facelift with these lightened-up and revamped old favorites.

2 cups fresh pineapple, cubed
¼ cup coconut milk
1 tablespoon dark rum
Dash of Angostura Bitters
1 pound firm peaches, halved and pitted
1 pound firm nectarines, halved and pitted
Maraschino cherry
2 mint sprigs

For the Fondue: In a blender, pulse the pineapple until smooth. Slowly stream in the coconut milk, rum, and bitters. Set aside.

For the Fruit: Place the peaches and nectarines, face down, on a very hot grill coated with oil or cooking spray. Grill for 3 minutes per side.

To Serve: Place the fruit with cut side facing up. Dip a spoon in the fondue and drizzle diagonally across the grilled fruit. Garnish with mint and cherry.

FALL

Only God Could Create Those Colors

Light Fare

Grilled Heart of Romaine with Creamy Coconut Chia Seed Dressing / 63

Massaged Kale & Pomegranate Salad with Grapefruit Ginger Dressing / 64

English Coconut Scones / 66

Coconut, Thyme, and Butternut Squash Chicken Soup / 68

Mains

Salsa Verde Coconut Rice / 69

Shrimp & Chow Mein Soba Bowl / 71

Oven Baked Coconut Sriracha Wings / 72

Za'atar & Lemon Shrimp Gyro with Cucumber Yogurt Dressing / 73

Lemongrass Shrimp Burger with Asian Slaw / 74

Creamy Coconut Brussels Sprout Gratin with Red Pepper Relish / 76

Shrimp & Grits / 78

Coconut Thai Shrimp Curry / 81

Sweet Potato & Ginger Latkes / 82

To Sip

Plantation Rum Punch / 83

Poached Pear Negroni / 84

The Sebastian Cocktail / 86

Spiced Rum & Ginger Sangria / 87

Sweet Endings

Rum-Laced Pumpkin Pie / 88

Plum, Honey, and Ginger Skillet Cake / 91

Grilled Heart of Romaine
with Creamy Coconut Chia Seed Dressing

Serves 4

A cozy cold weather salad with all the warm weather appeal. Seconds strongly recommended.

FOR THE GREENS
4 large hearts of Romaine, outer leaves
  discarded, halved
2 tablespoons coconut oil, divided
A pinch of salt and pepper

FOR THE DRESSING
½ cup coconut milk
1 tablespoon chia seeds
1 tablespoon lemon juice
¼ cup Greek yogurt
2 teaspoons agave

For the Dressing: In a small bowl, whisk to combine the lemon juice, salt, pepper, and agave. Then add in the Greek yogurt and whisk until it is evenly incorporated. Stream in the coconut milk so that it also becomes incorporated with dressing. Stir in the chia seeds and basil. Season to taste. Refrigerate.

For the Romaine: On a stove-top grill pan, over medium-high heat, add the coconut oil. Combine the remainder of the coconut oil with salt and pepper, and using a pastry brush, lightly baste the romaine with the oil mixture, paying attention to get some of this mixture in between the leaves. Place the romaine on the grill pan cut side down, and allow it to sear for about 3 minutes per side. The tips will become slightly charred; fret not. When deep grill marks have developed, flip and continue the process. When the romaine is grilled, sprinkle with parmesan cheese. Set aside on a platter and continue to grill the remaining heads.

To serve, top the romaine with dressing. Garnish with a wedge of lemon.

LIGHT FARE

Massaged Kale & Pomegranate Salad
with Grapefruit Ginger Dressing

Serves 2–4

A light, satisfying, colorful respite to starch-heavy autumnal fare.

Juice of 1 large red grapefruit
½ cup extra-virgin olive oil
2 teaspoons fresh ginger, minced
1 tablespoon raw honey
Salt and pepper to taste
4 cups raw kale leaves, triple-washed
¼ cup pomegranate seeds
Fresh parmesan for garnish (optional)

In a large bowl, whisk the grapefruit juice, olive oil, ginger, and honey. Season with a pinch of salt and pepper. To this dressing, add the kale leaves. Using your hands, toss the kale with the dressing and firmly crunch together with your hands. Repeat until all the kale is soft, dressed, and the texture has yielded to the warmth and brisk of your hands. Toss in the pomegranate seeds and garnish with freshly shaved parmesan.

English Coconut Scones

Makes 8–12

For reasons that warrant pardon, many folks across the pond would gently scoff at this here recipe. For one, the pronunciation of the word "scone" itself might elicit a slight side glance, as Brits often opt for a polite variation of "scawn." Then there's the butter. Unlike American scones, British bakers prefer using a soft fat, such as vegetable oil or lard, and less butter altogether in the dough. However, culinary politics aside, this recipe is replicated from the memory of Sunday afternoon baking with my mum. It's definitely not a purebred, as it skirts regional parameters. Nonetheless, it's inherently delicious and deceptively simple to make.

2 cups all-purpose flour
1½ cups coconut flour
1 tablespoon baking powder
½ teaspoon baking soda
¼ cup sugar
½ teaspoon salt
1 teaspoon lemon zest

1 stick (8 tablespoons) butter, cubed
  and very cold
2 cups buttermilk
1 cup full-fat coconut milk
1 egg, beaten, for egg wash
¼ cup coconut flakes

On a baking sheet lined with parchment paper or a silpat, place a small dusting of flour. In a large bowl, whisk dry ingredients (the flours, baking powder, baking soda, sugar, salt, and lemon zest). Using a pastry cutter, cut in the butter until the mixture resembles coarse crumbs. In a small bowl, combine the buttermilk and the coconut milk and gradually fold the milk mixture until the dough is well blended. Turn the dough out on the prepared baking sheet and very tenderly knead into a 1-inch thick rectangular shape. Place in the refrigerator and allow to chill for 45–60 minutes.

Following this, preheat oven to 425°F and make the egg wash. Using a serrated knife or a bench scraper, cut the dough into triangles, allowing your preference to determine the sizing. Space scones apart and brush with egg wash. Sprinkle the tops with coconut flakes and bake for 12–15 minutes. Serve warm with salted butter and home-stewed fruit preserve.

Coconut, Thyme, and Butternut Squash Chicken Soup

Serves 4-6

Full disclaimer: this soup is less than a representation of a winning recipe and more of an example of the comforts that soups can impart. My husband would proudly admit I should have written a book featuring just this soup. Why? It's what he ate as a kid in Jamaica, and decades later, no comfort food could ever dethrone his idea of a what a soup should be—loaded with veggies, creamy but not decadent, and simmered with a very perceivable pepper of aromatics. Honestly, this soup isn't my stand-out, but my husband is, so here it is.

2 tablespoons coconut oil

3 large cloves garlic

2 pounds boneless, skinless chicken breasts, cubed

2 teaspoons kosher salt

1 teaspoon black pepper

1 teaspoon allspice

2 tablespoons fresh thyme, divided

1 cup carrots, small dice

1 cup celery, small dice

1 cup Vidalia onions, small dice

1 cup butternut squash, diced

1 can full-fat coconut milk

2 quarts chicken stock

1 bay leaf

In a heavy bottom stock pot over medium heat, add the coconut oil and garlic. Allow the garlic to sweat until fragrant. Meanwhile, season the chicken breast with salt, pepper, allspice, and half of the thyme. Add the chicken breast to the pot and allow to brown about 3 minutes per side. When the chicken is browned and a noticeable amount of fond (brown bits) has developed at the bottom of the pot, add the carrots, celery, onions, squash, and a splash of coconut milk. Using a wooden spoon, scrape up the brown bits and incorporate into the veg. Allow the vegetables and poultry to cook for 5 minutes, still on medium heat. Add the stock and the bay leaf and cook for another 20–25 minutes. Add the rest of the coconut milk and the remainder of the fresh thyme and simmer on low heat for 3–5 minutes. Remove the bay leaf. Season to taste.

Salsa Verde Coconut Rice

Cilantro lime rice takes a back seat to this upbeat recipe that hones in on the effortless verve of the tomatillo. Enterprise takes this unassuming dish to the next level and reinforces this main, as an affordable and creative alternative to Mexican rice.

1 cup coconut milk
2 cups long-grained rice, rinsed
1 teaspoon butter
4 cloves garlic, peeled
3 medium tomatillos, quartered
½ small yellow onion, roughly chopped
½ bunch cilantro, roughly chopped
4 stalks green onion (including the whites), chopped
3 tablespoons lime juice
1 tablespoon coconut oil
Kosher salt and coarse ground black pepper, to taste

In a medium saucepan, combine the coconut milk with 1½ cup water, add the rice, butter, and salt. Bring to a boil, stir, then immediately reduce heat to low. Cook covered for another 15–20 minutes. Turn off heat, fluff the rice with a fork. Set aside.

In a food processor, pulse all the ingredients for the salsa verde: garlic, tomatillos, onion, cilantro, green onion, lime juice, and coconut oil, until well combined. Season to taste.

Transfer the rice to a large bowl then fold in the salsa verde. It should be completely green. Season with salt and black pepper and drizzle with coconut oil if desired.

MAINS

Shrimp & Chow Mein Soba Bowl

Serves 4

The nutty heft of Japanese buckwheat noodles are gathered and tossed about a bevy of everyday ingredients, producing a proud bowl of lip-smacking glory and, if nothing else, a newcomer to the weeknight dinner rotation.

3 tablespoons sesame oil, divided
1 pound shrimp (any size) peeled, deveined, tails removed
2 teaspoons Chinese Five Spice
Zest of 1 lime
1 teaspoon soy sauce
1 tablespoon rice vinegar
1 pound soba noodles
6 cloves garlic, minced

2 tablespoons ginger, minced
1 large yellow onion, sliced
3 stalks celery, bias cut (including leaves)
3 large carrots, bias cut
2 stalks scallions, bias cut
Black sesame seeds to garnish (optional)

In a wok, heat 1 tablespoon of sesame oil until hot but not smoking. Add the shrimp, Chinese Five Spice, lime zest, soy sauce, and rice vinegar. Sauté, stirring occasionally until the shrimp is cooked and not translucent, with no visible blue. Remove the shrimp and set aside.

In a large stock pot with rapidly boiling unsalted water, add the noodles and stir to separate. Reduce heat to a simmer and allow the noodles to cook for 5–8 minutes. In the sink, ready the colander and prepare a large bowl of cold (not iced) water. The noodles should be cooked all the way through and not have that al-dente texture characteristic of other typical pastas. Drain the soba in the colander and swiftly transfer them to the cold water. Following this, firmly massage the noodles to remove the excess starch. Once again, drain in the colander. Set aside.

In the wok, add the remainder of the sesame oil, garlic, and ginger, and sauté until fragrant. Add the vegetables and cook until they are tender but not overly soft, about 3–5 minutes. Working in batches, delicately incorporate the soba noodles and shrimp. Leave the vegetables and noodles on the heat until the soba noodles have warmed completely. Add the scallions. Garnish with black sesame seeds.

Oven Baked Coconut Sriracha Wings

Serves 4-6

Not even the most seasoned of palates would be able to discriminate if these wings were deep fried and dredged in MSG, or in this case, oven-baked with the spices of the orient.

4 ounces reduced fat coconut milk

¼ cup Sriracha

2 tablespoons soy sauce

2 teaspoons brown sugar

2 tablespoons rice vinegar

1 tablespoon kosher salt

1 tablespoon coarse ground black
   pepper

5 cloves garlic, minced

1 tablespoon fresh ginger, grated

1 teaspoon red pepper flakes

2 pounds chicken wings, separated
   at joints

5 sprigs green onion, bias cut through
   greens and whites

2 teaspoons black sesame seeds

Make the Sauce: In a small saucepan over medium heat, combine the coconut milk, Sriracha, soy sauce, brown sugar, and vinegar. Whisk until the sugar is dissolved. Reduce the heat to low and allow the sauce to slightly thicken.

For the Wings: Preheat oven to 375°F.

In a small bowl, combine the salt, pepper, garlic, ginger, and chili flakes. Set aside.

Lightly coat a baking sheet with cooking spray. Place the wings on the baking sheet and evenly toss with seasoning blend. Bake for 10 minutes.

Remove the wings and coat with the sauce. Using tongs, ensure that each piece is coated in the sauce. Return to the oven and bake for another 10 minutes. Repeat this process one last time. Allow the wings to cool and garnish with black sesame seeds and scallions.

FALL

Za'atar & Lemon Shrimp Gyro
with Cucumber Yogurt Dressing

Serves 4

The flavors of the Mideast take center stage in this upbeat spin on fish tacos. A flatbread drizzled with olive oil and a dash of the borrowed spices, makes this a crowd pleaser with added nutritional oomph.

3 large cloves garlic, minced
Juice and zest of 2 lemons
   (reserve zest)
2 tablespoons ׀ 2 teaspoons extra-
   virgin olive oil, plus more for
   drizzling
1 tablespoon + 1 teaspoon za'atar
2 pounds large shrimp, peeled and
   deveined, tails removed

½ cup plain Greek yogurt
1 cup cucumber, diced
1 teaspoon kosher salt
1 teaspoon freshly milled black
   pepper
4 rounds of pita
¼ cup feta cheese
1 small red onion, sliced
Salt and pepper to taste

For the Shrimp: In a large bowl, combine the garlic, lemon juice, 2 tablespoons oil, and 1 tablespoon of za'atar spice, and briskly whisk until it is well combined. Add the shrimp and allow it to marinate for 10 minutes. Meanwhile, make the dressing. In a bowl combine the yogurt, lemon zest, cucumber, and 2 teaspoons of olive oil, until evenly combined. Season to taste and refrigerate. In a sauté pan over high heat add the marinated shrimp and allow it to char for about 5 minutes per side. Remove from heat and set aside.

For the Flatbread: Drizzle one side of the pita with olive oil and sprinkle with 1 teaspoon of za'atar. On a hot griddle, toast (seasoned side down) for 1 minute. Keep toasted bread covered.

Assemble by placing the shrimp atop the pita, then the dressing, followed by red onions and a sprinkle of feta cheese.

Lemongrass Shrimp Burger with Asian Slaw

Serves 4

East meets West in this seafood-inspired staple. With a double burst of the highly aromatic, citrusy herb lemongrass, this burger hones in on the energy & tangy characteristic of the flavors of orient. For an even healthier option, nix the bun and serve the burger over a side of dark, leafy greens, tossed in a simple dressing of lemon juice and olive oil.

1 bunch lemongrass
2 pounds shrimp, any size, peeled and
   deveined
2 tablespoons scallions, chopped
1 teaspoon lemon zest
1 egg, beaten
1 cup breadcrumbs
Salt and pepper to taste
¼ cup + 1 tablespoon sesame oil,
   divided
1 tablespoon rice vinegar

Juice of 1 lime
2 teaspoons brown sugar
2 tablespoons fish sauce
2 teaspoons fresh ginger, peeled and
   minced
1 thinly sliced medium red bell pepper
3 cups thinly sliced Napa cabbage
2 cups thinly sliced purple cabbage
4 stalks bias cut green onions
Salt & pepper to taste
4 rolls of choice

For the Slaw: In a medium-sized bowl, whisk ¼ cup of the sesame oil, vinegar, fish sauce, lime juice, and brown sugar until well combined and the sugar is dissolved. Then toss the remaining ingredients until everything is well coated with the dressing. Season to taste with salt and pepper and store chilled in an airtight container.

For the Burgers: Peel and rough chop the outer layers of the lemongrass. Reserve the soft interior. In a medium sauce pan, boil the outer layers with the shrimp for about 3 minutes. Drain, then discard the outer lemongrass layers and allow the shrimp to cool. Give the shrimp a very quick chop. Large pieces of the shrimp should be visible.

Finely chop the soft interior of the lemongrass. In a large bowl, mix the lemongrass, shrimp, scallions, and lemon zest. Then incorporate the egg, breadcrumbs, and salt and pepper.

Using your hands, form 4 patties. Sauté, 2 at a time, in the sesame oil until both sides are golden brown. Drain on paper towels and serve on rolls with Asian slaw.

Creamy Coconut Brussels Sprout Gratin with Red Pepper Relish

Serves 6–8

Here's to a dish that is sure to dethrone most, if not all, of the typical Thanksgiving sides. Inventive but not avant-garde, approachable but not predictable. This gratin has all the makings of a year-after-year holiday hit, and best of all, it's a casserole-esque dish that can be made ramekin-ready, for individual serving without struggle.

FOR THE GRATIN
1 tablespoon butter
2 pound Brussels sprouts, washed, trimmed, and finely shredded
1 cup coconut milk
½ cup heavy cream
¾ cup freshly grated Parmigiano-Reggiano cheese
1 teaspoon salt
1 teaspoon coarse ground black pepper
Dash of red pepper flakes

FOR THE TOPPING
2 cups Panko breadcrumbs
¼ cup freshly grated Parmigiano-Reggiano cheese
1 tablespoon flat-leaf parsley, finely chopped

FOR THE RED PEPPER RELISH
2 large red bell peppers, cored and diced small
1 teaspoon extra-virgin olive oil
⅓ cup shallots, diced small
¼ cup red wine vinegar
2 tablespoons sugar

Preheat oven to 350°F. Butter a glass bakeware dish or an oven-safe nonstick frying pan. On high heat, bring a large pot of salted water to a boil. Add the shredded Brussels sprouts to the salted water and cook for about 8–10 minutes. While the Brussels sprouts are cooking, whisk together the coconut milk, heavy cream, cheese, and spices, in the prepared baking dish. Then assemble the breadcrumbs by combining the panko, parsley, and cheese (if you are preparing single-serve portions in individual ramekins, mix the milk and spices in a large bowl, with ample space to hold the Brussels sprouts). When the sprouts are completed, drain and transfer to the prepared baking dish or large bowl. Stir to combine the Brussels sprouts with the milk, cheese, and spice mixture. Evenly top with the prepared breadcrumbs and bake for 30–35 minutes.

When the gratin is baking, make the red pepper relish. In a small sauté pan, add the olive oil and sauté the shallots until soft, fragrant, and translucent. Add the red peppers, and sauté until softened. Stir in the sugar, then the vinegar, and cook until most of the liquid has evaporated. Remove from heat and allow to cool. When the gratin is golden brown with soft creamy bubbles, remove from the oven, allow to cool for 10 minutes, and top with jewel-toned relish.

Shrimp & Grits

Serves 4

No longer sequestered to the South, or breakfast, for that matter, Shrimp & Grits has made a triumphant—and some may argue, permanent—placement on the lunch and dinner menus of many big cities. For the low-country home cook, however, grits have always been an underwhelming staple, now they're just more refined.

6 cups water

3 gloves garlic (2 minced, 1 whole)

1½ tablespoons salt

1 tablespoon pepper

1½ cups stone ground grits

4 tablespoons butter

1 cup parmesan cheese, freshly grated

4 slices thick-cut bacon, chopped into 1-inch pieces

2 pounds shrimp, peeled and deveined, patted dry

1 medium tomato (about ½ cup), chopped

Juice of 1 lemon

Scallions & cilantro, chopped for garnish

Bring the water to a boil, then add 1 whole garlic clove, salt, and pepper. Reduce heat to medium, remove the garlic, and slowly add grits, whisking occasionally until the grits are completely cooked, for about 25 minutes. Reduce heat to very low. Whisk in the butter until the grits are ethereally smooth and creamy. Fold in the cheese.

Over medium high heat, in a skillet, add the bacon and render the fat. Ready a paper towel lined plate. Using a slotted spoon, remove the bacon, place on the paper towel, and reserve the fat in the pan. Add the minced garlic and quickly sauté in the bacon fat until fragrant. Add the shrimp and cook until the shrimp is firm and has lost its blue hue. Add the tomatoes and lemon juice. Season to taste. Sauté for 3–5 minutes. Turn off heat. Spoon the grits into a serving bowl, top with shrimp, garnish with scallions and cilantro; serve immediately.

Coconut Thai Shrimp Curry

Serves 4

Jasmine rice perfumed with curry leaves. Colossal shrimp simmered in creamy coconut peanut sauce. A riot of fresh vegetables. And aromatics bursting with flavors from the orient make this dish a household staple, the world over.

2 cups Jasmine rice
1 tablespoon butter
2 teaspoons salt
2 stems curry leaves, about 16 leaves
1 pound jumbo shrimp, peeled, deveined, tail-on
1 teaspoon salt
1 teaspoon black pepper
4 tablespoons sesame oil, divided
4 cloves garlic, minced
1 teaspoon red pepper flakes
1 tablespoon fresh ginger, minced

1 small yellow onion, sliced
1 small carrot, peeled and bias cut
1 red bell pepper, sliced
1 orange bell pepper, sliced
1 cup coconut milk
2 tablespoons peanut butter
¼ cup fish sauce
1 tablespoon brown sugar
Juice of 1 lime
2 tablespoons Thai basil, chopped
4 whole cilantro sprigs
2 sprigs green onion, bias cut

Add 3 cups of water, the rice, butter, and salt to a pot on medium-low heat. Add the curry leaves. Cover and allow to cook on low for 15–18 minutes. Do not stir. Remove from heat and use a fork to remove the curry leaves and fluff the rice. Set aside.

In a medium bowl, combine the shrimp, salt, and pepper, half of the sesame oil, half the garlic, chili flakes, and half the ginger. Marinade for 10–15 minutes.

In a wok or large skillet, heat the remainder of the sesame oil over medium-high, then add the onions, the remainder of the garlic and ginger, and sauté for 2–3 minutes. Add the peppers and carrots; sauté for another minute or so. Add the marinated shrimp and cook for about 4–5 minutes.

In a small bowl, whisk together the coconut milk, peanut butter, fish sauce, and brown sugar. Pour this mixture over the shrimp and simmer for 5–7 minutes. Turn off the heat. Squeeze the lime juice over the shrimp. Stir in the basil. Serve over curry scented rice and garnish with cilantro sprigs.

NOTE: Curry leaves are obscenely affordable and easily freezable, so don't fret if you end up with a large, ample bunch for a dollar and change. These leaves will serve you in good stead, adding depth and flavor to a range of dishes—from slow cooker stews to oven baked meats—year round.

Sweet Potato & Ginger Latkes

Serves 2-4

This twist on a Jewish staple does not buck its traditional roots, rather, it embraces them. The sweet potato plays on the natural sweet notes of the ginger. And the inclusion of red pepper flakes adds docile heat without being overwhelming.

1 pound sweet potatoes, peeled and largely grated
1 tablespoon fresh ginger, grated
¼ cup all-purpose flour
¼ cup flat leaf parsley, roughly chopped
2 eggs, beaten
1 teaspoon salt
½ teaspoon red pepper flakes
½ cup canola oil

In a large bowl, combine all the ingredients. In a large sauté pan, heat the oil until hot but not smoking. Using an ice cream scoop, scoop the mixture and use your hands to shape and flatten slightly. Put into the pan and flatten using the back side of a spatula. Reduce heat to medium and cook for about 2 minutes per side. The latkes should be golden brown. Drain on plate lined with paper towels.

Plantation Rum Punch

Serves a couple or a crowd

Centuries ago, in Barbados, this wondrously adaptable recipe was frequently employed in plantation houses. To this day, the rhythmic ratio is enshrined both as a cultural relic of a bygone era, as well as a culinary icon that island folk still rely on. Its ease and reliability has traveled throughout the Caribbean and it's one of those storied recipes passed down, from one generation to the next by word-of-mouth. Traditionally, lime, sugar, Bajan Rum, and water were the ingredients. However, in the end, the success of any well-balanced punch made using this recipe depends more on the ratios rather than its components.

Here's the ratio recipe: One Sour. Two Sweet. Three Strong. Four Weak.

An Autumnal Adapation: Grapefruit Juice. Ginger Simple Syrup. Dark Rum. Seltzer Water.

TO SIP

Poached Pear Negroni

Makes 1 pitcher

The end of the year presents itself as the most perfect time for pear-poaching. This ultra-gentle, stovetop cooking method allows the pears to uphold their shape yet relent their firmness. The taste of nondescript, less-than-desirable pears are masked behind the sultry sweet of the poaching liquid, in this case honey, ginger, and red vermouth. And best of all, poached pears are champions of versatility. Here the confidence of a negroni—that classic, siren-red, Italian cocktail—is tamed but not muted by the pears' preparation and presence. In the end, this recipe equips you with all the makings of a stellar cocktail as well as dessert-worthy leftovers.

1 tablespoon honey
1 teaspoon ginger, freshly grated
2 cups red vermouth, divided
2 firm d'anjou pears, peeled
1 cup dry gin
½ cup Campari
1 medium navel orange

In a saucepan, over medium heat, combine the honey, ginger, and 1 cup of the vermouth. Stir until the honey has dissolved into the other ingredients. Add the pears, cover the saucepan, and cook for 25 minutes. Remove the saucepan from heat and allow both the pears and the poaching liquid to cool. Meanwhile, take a vegetable peeler and in one continuous motion, peel the entire zest off of a navel orange. If needed (or desired), trim the edges off the peel for a clean and neat appearance. Once cooled, place one or two pears at the bottom of a martini pitcher. Measure ¼ cup of the poaching liquid and strain into the pitcher. Next, add the gin, the Campari, the vermouth, and stir gently to mix the elements together. Add the orange peel. In four rocks glasses or chilled coupe glasses, filled ¼ of the way with ice, pour about 3–4 ounces (a little shy of half of a cup) of this now-poached pear negroni into each rocks glass. From here, make another round.

The Sebastian Cocktail

Serves 2

This libation is an aggregate of the ingredients that Americans have come to adore about its bordering neighbor in the South West. The tequila, which is a derivative from agave, gives this drink balance as well as promise. The dark rum creates a long and lingering warm mid-palate, and the ginger beer plays on the contours of both liquors. The subtle saccharine notes of the agave gently blunts some (but not all) of the acidity in the lime juice. Altogether this a multi-season, well-balanced cocktail, one that is sure to please even the most discerning of palates.

1 teaspoon agave
⅓ cup tequila
¼ cup dark rum
Dash of Angostura Bitters
1 lime, juiced
½ cup ounces Crabbie's Ginger Beer
2 cloves candied ginger, uncrystallized

In a cocktail shaker filled halfway with ice, add the agave, tequila, dark rum, bitters, and lime juice. Shake vigorously. Pour into a chilled martini glass and top with the ginger beer. Garnish with candied ginger speared through a beverage skewer.

FALL

Spiced Rum & Ginger Sangria

Serves 4

Here, fortified dark rum is mingled with red wine for a lively libation bursting with all of the uncanny energy of winter citrus.

⅓ cup water
⅓ cup brown sugar
2 inches ginger root, rough chopped
1 cup dark rum
2 cinnamon sticks
3 cloves
1 teaspoon nutmeg, grated
1 (12-ounce) bottle non-alcoholic ginger beer
Half a bottle of mid-range Malbec
1 orange, sliced
1 lime, sliced
1 tangerine, sliced
4 kumquats (to garnish)

In a small saucepan, make the brown sugar ginger simple syrup by bringing the water, brown sugar, and ginger, to a boil. Meanwhile in an ample enough bowl, add the rum along with cinnamon, cloves, and nutmeg. When the simple syrup has boiled and cooled (a process that should take about 20–30 minutes), add that simple syrup to the bowl containing spice-infused rum. Stir to combine then strain into glass pitcher. To this, add the ginger beer, red wine, and fruit. Refrigerate to serve chilled. Garnish with a skewered kumquat.

TO SIP

Rum-Laced Pumpkin Pie

Serves 6–8

This twist on the perennial Thanksgiving classic is not for the faint of heart. The warm spices, viscous molasses, and dark rum crescendo into a decadent delight, one which truly allows anyone enjoying this treat to relax into the flavors of the season. This pie is best served day-old, as the ribbons of flavors have time to meld.

BASIC PIE CRUST
2½ cups all-purpose flour
1 teaspoon salt
1 teaspoon granulated sugar
2 sticks unsalted butter, cubed and chilled
¼ cup iced water

LACED WHIPPED CREAM
1 cup heavy cream
3 tablespoons powdered sugar
1 tablespoon dark rum
1 teaspoon pure vanilla extract

THE FILLING
1 (15-ounce) can pumpkin puree
½ cup light brown sugar
¼ cup maple syrup
½ teaspoon ground cinnamon
¼ teaspoon fresh ginger, grated
¼ teaspoon ground nutmeg
½ teaspoon kosher salt
¼ cup molasses
3 large eggs, lightly beaten
1 cup heavy cream
¼ cup dark rum

In a food processor: Pulse the flour, salt, and sugar. Add the butter and blend for 60 seconds. It should resemble coarse corn meal or be pea-sized. Slowly stream in the water and combine for another minute. When the dough is incorporated, divide into half and turn onto a workspace lined with plastic wrap and press into a flattened disk. Refrigerate for at least 1 hour, because if the dough fails to rest, it will shrink as it bakes.

By hand: In a very large, wide bowl, whisk the flour, salt, and sugar. Dot the flour mixture with cubes of butter and employing a pastry cutter, mash the butter into the flour mixture until combined. When this mixture is pea-sized, drizzle the cold water and combine using a rubber spatula. If more water is required, add it using a tablespoon at a time. When the dough is formed, divide into half, and turn onto a workspace lined with plastic wrap and press into a flattened disk. Refrigerate for at least 1 hour, because if the dough fails to rest it will shrink as it bakes.

Preheat oven to 400°F degrees.

To Roll the Dough: Remove the dough from the refrigerator and let temper for a few minutes. Unwrap the dough on a clean and generously floured surface. Using a floured rolling pin, press gently down on the middle of the dough and roll outward—always roll dough from the center outwards. Continue this process, lifting and rotating the dough. Flour the counter as needed to avoid sticking. Be patient with yourself, dough tends to be temperamental and a bench scraper makes easy work of lifting dough that, despite heavy flouring, persist to cling to the workspace. Roll the dough to a 12–13 inch circle, which is the standard size pie tin. And using your rolling pin, transfer the dough onto your pie pan. Press the dough gently into the pan, ensuring it is evenly distributed and centered. Fold the overhanging dough under and decoratively crimp the edges with your fingers. Refrigerate for 20 minutes.

Remove the pan from the refrigerator and line the crust with foil or parchment paper and fill ¾ of the way full with beans or any other pie weight and bake for 15 minutes. After the time has elapsed, remove foil and weights and rotate pie and bake for an addition 5 minutes.

Prepare the Filling: Reduce the oven temperature to 325°F. In the bowl of stand mixer fitted with the whisk attachment, incorporate the pumpkin, sugar, maple syrup, spices, molasses, eggs, cream, and rum, until smooth and very well combined. With a sieve atop another bowl, pass this mixture through strainer using a rubber spatula to remove any clumps. From there, pour the filling into the baked pie shell. Bake for 45–50 minutes until the filling is set in the middle. Set aside allow to cool completely and serve with the rum-laced whipped cream.

For the Whipped Cream: In the bowl of the stand mixer fitted with the whisk attachment add the cream and beat on medium speed for 60 seconds. Then, add the sugar, rum, and vanilla, and beat on medium-high speed until fluffy and soft peaks form.

> **NOTE:** When making pastry dough, the more apparent the butter, the flakier the crust. Temperature also plays a major role in the formation of a flaky crust, hence why butter and water should be as cold as possible. In addition, if you are not using the food processor, avoid overworking the dough by hand since your body heat may compromise the cold temperature.

Plum, Honey, and Ginger Skillet Cake

Serves 4–8

This adaptable dessert (think kumquats instead of plums during the winter citrus season) with prize-worthy looks and no exacting ratios, will disarm even the most baking-phobic of home cooks.

1 stick unsalted butter
1 cup all-purpose flour
½ cup sugar
2 teaspoons baking powder
Pinch of salt
1 cup milk
¼ cup ginger root, freshly grated
½ cup honey
1 teaspoon vanilla extract
1 pound plums, sliced into ¼-inch thick segments

Preheat oven to 350°F. Place the stick of butter in a cast-iron skillet, and place the skillet in the oven for 6–8 minutes. In a large bowl, whisk to combine the dry ingredients (flour, sugar, baking powder, and salt). Remove the skillet from the oven, gently lapping the sides of the skillet with the melted butter, and add the melted butter to the dry ingredients. Stir to combine. Add the milk, ginger, honey, and vanilla extract and fold until evenly combined. Pour the mixture back into the warm, buttered skillet and arrange plums on top, leaving a little space between the perimeter of the plums and the rim of the skillet. Place the skillet in the oven and bake for one hour, until the cake is golden brown and there is no residue on the cake tester. Allow the skillet to cool on wire rack. Serve warm with any cool and creamy accoutrement: ice cream, whipped cream, or crème fraiche.

WINTER

A Stiff Back; A Harbinger of Hope

Light Fare

Coconut Spiced Cashews / 94

Bacon Bourbon Shrimp Butter with Pomegranate Seeds / 96

Roasted Cauliflower Coconut Tabbouleh / 97

Ginger, Almond, and Matcha Tea Biscotti / 99

Cheese Board with Champagne and Ginger Chutney / 100

Black Fig & Ginger Compote / 102

Carrot, Coconut, and Cardamom Bisque / 103

Coconut Stuffed French Toast / 104

Mains

Grilled Cheese with Coconut Butter, Frisee, and Blood Orange / 106

Shrimp, Artichoke, and Saffron Risotto / 108

Shrimp Dumplings & Napa Cabbage Broth Bowl / 110

Blackened Shrimp Mac n' Cheese / 112

To Sip

Blood Orange, Mint, and Ginger Margarita / 113

Clementine Honey Sparkler / 114

Ponche a Crème / 115

Champagne Ginger Sidecar / 116

Sweet Endings

Triple Ginger-Ginger Snaps / 117

Rum-Laced Bundt Cake / 118

Boozy Coconut Bread Pudding / 120

Coconut Spiced Cashews

Serves 1-4

Appetites run high for these made-in-20-minutes morsels. These cashews are a cluster of contradictions, in that they are simultaneously salty, sweet, spicy, and wondrously crunchy. They're incomparably addictive, but also high in iron and potassium and all that good fat.

2 tablespoons coconut oil
½ cup light brown sugar
¼ cup coconut water
1 teaspoon chili powder
1 teaspoon red pepper flakes
1 teaspoon kosher salt
1½ cups whole cashews
¼ cup unsweetened coconut flakes

Preheat oven to 350°F. Brush a rimmed baking sheet with half of the coconut oil. In a saucepan, over medium heat, dissolve the sugar in the coconut water. Increase heat and boil without stirring until the mixture is darker and thicker, with large rolling bubbles. This should take roughly 5 minutes. Remove the saucepan from the heat and quickly add chili powder, the remainder of the coconut oil, red pepper flakes, and salt. Add the cashews and stir, using a rubber spatula, until all the nuts are well coated with the syrup and spice mixture. Add the coconut flakes to the cashews and stir until all the cashews are coated with coconuts. Transfer to baking sheet and spread apart the nuts. Bake for 9–10 minutes until the nuts are browned and highly fragrant. Cool, break apart, and store in an airtight container for 1 week, that is, if they last a week.

Bacon Bourbon Shrimp Butter
with Pomegranate Seeds

Serves 6–8

Bacon wrapped shrimp has been ousted by this stellar twist. This spread makes for the ultimate holiday hors d'oeuvre. The jeweled specs from the pomegranate not only give this butter magazine-worthy looks but their bright tartness cuts the fat of the bacon. It is best served smeared over a crusty, bias-cut, butter-toasted baguette.

1 teaspoon extra-virgin olive oil
1 clove garlic, minced
½ pound shrimp, peeled, deveined, tails removed
4 tablespoons bourbon, divided
6 ounces (about 4 slices) bacon, diced
4 tablespoons butter
1 teaspoon fresh thyme, finely chopped
Salt and pepper to taste
Seeds of 1 large pomegranate

In a small sauté pan or cast iron skillet, over medium-high, heat the olive oil and sauté minced garlic until fragrant. Add the shrimp and allow them to gently char for about 2 minutes per side. Add an ounce of the bourbon and allow the alcohol to cook out for about 1 minute. Season to taste, remove from skillet, and roughly chop the shrimp. Transfer the shrimp to a medium sized bowl. In the same sauté pan or skillet, cook the bacon and sauté for 5–6 minutes until the bacon is crispy. Remove with slotted spoon and place on a paper towel–lined plate. Roughly chop the bacon and place it in the bowl with the shrimp. To this bowl, add the butter, bourbon, and chopped fresh thyme. Season with a pinch of salt and pepper. Using a fork, vigorously combine all the elements. During this process, the shrimp should become more macerated, but still very visible. On a sheet of parchment paper or plastic wrap, place the butter mixture and fold the paper over and roll into a cylindrical log shape. With the ends of the log tightly twisted, refrigerate until solid. Serve with toasted French bread and garnish with fresh thyme and pomegranate seeds.

Roasted Cauliflower Coconut Tabbouleh

Serves 4-6

This grain-free version of the popular Mediterranean salad made with bulgur wheat, is hearty and delicious enough to be enjoyed on its own. While raw cauliflower rice could be employed, the roasting gives this tabbouleh an uncanny sweetness and depth.

1 large head cauliflower, side leaves removed

4 tablespoons coconut oil, divided

2 tablespoons freshly squeezed lemon juice

1 tablespoon kosher salt

½ tablespoon coarse ground black pepper

2 cups cucumbers, small dice

1 pint grape tomatoes, halved

1 bunch curly parsley, chopped

½ cup fresh mint, chopped

Preheat oven to 350°F.

For the Cauliflower: Trim all the leaves from the stem. Take a cookie cutter, one that is the same circumference as the stem of the cauliflower, and insert it on the base of the cauliflower, so that the cauliflower is able to stand upright freely. Rub the head of the cauliflower with half of the coconut oil and sprinkle with salt and pepper. Bake for 30 minutes, until the head of the cauliflower is golden brown. Allow to cool. When cooled, use a sharp chef's knife to shave off toasted florets. Reserve the roasted stem for making vegetable stock.

Make the Dressing: In a large bowl, whisk together the lemon juice, remainder of the coconut oil, salt, and pepper. To that, add the cucumbers, tomatoes, parsley, and mint, and stir to combine. Add the roasted cauliflower last, and evenly incorporate.

> **NOTE:** There are numerous ways to roast a cauliflower. This method requires a bit more enterprise and tenacity but it yields a product that is unfailingly uniform and crispy.

Ginger, Almond, and Matcha Tea Biscotti

Serves 4-6

These twice-baked Italian cookies pack a one-two punch. The ginger is a powerful anti-inflammatory and aids in digestion and the chlorophyll-rich matcha tea contains the antioxidant polyphenol, which protects against heart disease.

1 cup granulated sugar
1½ sticks butter, melted
1 teaspoon fresh ginger, grated
¼ teaspoon ground cardamom
2½ tablespoons matcha tea powder
1 teaspoon almond extract
1 teaspoon pure vanilla extract
1 cup whole almonds, toasted, cooled, and chopped
3 eggs
3 cups all-purpose flour, sifted
2 teaspoons baking powder
½ teaspoon kosher salt

In a large bowl combine the sugar, butter, ginger, cardamom, matcha, and extracts. Following this, add the almonds and eggs. Lastly, stir in the flour, baking powder, and salt, until well combined.

Allow the dough to chill for 30 minutes. Preheat oven to 350°F. Using wet hands, halve the dough and place on a large ungreased baking sheet. Bake for 30 minutes, remove tray from oven, and allow the dough to cool for 15 minutes on wire rack. Using a serrated knife, cut dough in ¾-inch slices. On a clean baking sheet, arrange biscotti (cut side down) and bake for another 25–30 minutes, until golden brown. Transfer to a wire rack to allow it to cool. Note that the flavors in biscotti deepen with time, therefore it's best to make a day or two ahead and store in an airtight container.

LIGHT FARE

Cheese Board with Champagne and Ginger Chutney

Serves as many as you'd like

Not inherently American or West Indian because at any social soiree the world over, there's likely to be some variant of a cheese platter. And because cheeseboards are predictable and that popular, I tend to subscribe to a heuristic that the edible contents should be carried on the most appealing and interesting of possible vehicles—a mirror, a slab of salt, a window pane—anything that would add a touch of whim and contrast. There is no hard and fast rule of cheeseboard assembly, except that of proportions: there should be one pound of cheese for every 4–5 people. Barring the actual cheese, nuts, meats, seeds, spreads, herbs, as well as a riot of color and textural variety, are key to composition.

FOR THE CHUTNEY
1 tablespoon butter
1 cup shallots, finely minced
2 cups champagne
⅓ cup fresh ginger, peeled and minced
½ cup firm green grapes
1 cup firmly packed brown sugar
¼ cup golden raisins
1 teaspoon salt

In a heavy bottom saucepan, melt butter until slightly nutty then add the shallots and sauté for a few minutes until soft and translucent. Add the champagne, then add the ginger root, grapes, brown sugar, golden raisins, and salt. Over medium-high heat, bring the mixture to a boil, stirring occasionally, for about 35 minutes until the mixture has thickened. When the chutney has cooled, spoon it into a glass jar with tight fitting lid.

To assemble the cheese board: choose one or two cheeses from each dominant category and arrange as artfully as possible.

Aged: Comte, Gouda, Cheddar, Gruyere

Soft: Brie, Camembert, Smoked Ricotta, Fontina

Firm: Mimolette, Garrotxa, Manchego, Parmigiano-Reggiano

Blue: Stilton, Roqueford, Gorgonzola, Maytag Blue

Black Fig & Ginger Compote

Serves 4-6

Issue store-bought fig jam its walking papers, by creating a batch of this intriguing spread dynamic enough to be used in a host of preparations, from glazing meats to topping off your morning granola.

1 pound fresh mission figs, rinsed, stems removed, quartered
3 tablespoons brown sugar
½ cup champagne vinegar
½ cup balsamic vinegar
1 tablespoon ginger, freshly grated
1 vanilla bean pod, sliced in half lengthwise
½ teaspoon salt
½ teaspoon pepper

In a saucepan, on medium-high heat, combine the figs, sugar, and vinegars. Bring to a boil, then reduce heat to medium-low. Add the ginger, then using the tip of a sharp paring knife, scrape the seeds from the vanilla bean into the saucepan. Add salt and pepper, and cook for 30 minutes until the mixture has thickened and the volume has reduced. Following this, place the fig mixture in a blender or food processor, and pulse until smooth.

Carrot, Coconut, and Cardamom Bisque

Serves 4-6

Here's a soup that challenges you to rethink how a simple, everyday ingredient like carrots could be satisfying, engaging, and attention-getting, with a little help from friends.

½ tablespoon coconut oil

½ tablespoon unsalted butter

3 gloves garlic, smashed

2 teaspoons fresh ginger, grated

1 large Vidalia onion, chopped

½ cup fennel, chopped

2 large leeks, whites only (reserve the green portion for vegetable stock), sliced

1 tablespoon kosher salt

3 stalks celery, chopped

½ cup Macintosh apple, seeded and diced

2 pounds large carrots, peeled and roughly chopped

½ teaspoon ground cardamom

1 quart vegetable stock

½ cup coconut milk

¼ cup heavy cream

¼ cup dry white wine

½ tablespoon coarse ground black pepper

1 tablespoon good quality maple syrup

In a large, heavy-bottomed pot, melt the coconut oil and butter. To that, add the garlic, ginger, onions, fennel, and leeks, and sauté until slightly fragrant. Sprinkle with a pinch of kosher salt. Stir in the celery, apples, and carrots, and allow to cook for 5–7 minutes, until the vegetables are soft. Stir in the cardamom. Pour in the stock and bring to a slow boil. Reduce heat and simmer for 25–30 minutes.

Working in batches, transfer the soup to a blender and process until smooth without any lumps. When all the soup is blended, return to the pot and gradually incorporate the coconut milk, heavy cream, and wine. Season to taste. Garnish with fennel frond and drizzle of maple syrup.

Coconut Stuffed French Toast

Serves 3–5

Stale, dry bread is saturated back to life by creamy coconut milk and a smattering of warm spices. Coconut infused cream cheese forms the core. As if French toast needed any more reason to be star of your morning.

1 cup coconut milk, divided

1 tablespoon + 1 teaspoon coconut extract

4 ounces plain cream cheese

½ cup unsweetened coconut flakes, divided

6 eggs

½ cup milk

1 tablespoon pure vanilla extract

½ teaspoon ground cinnamon

½ teaspoon ground nutmeg

Pinch of salt

½ stick butter

1 teaspoon salt

6 slices day-old egg bread (challah or brioche)

Maple syrup for serving

In a small bowl, combine half of coconut milk, 1 teaspoon of the coconut extract, and the pinch of salt, with the cream cheese. Add ¼ cup of the coconut flakes. Set aside.

In an ample size bowl, whisk to combine the eggs, other half of the coconut milk, ½ cup of milk, vanilla extract, remaining coconut extract, teaspoon of salt, and spices.

In a 9 × 13 glass rectangular baking dish, lay flat the bread and pour the egg mixture over the bread and allow to soak for about 10 minutes.

Generously butter a stove-top or electric griddle on medium-high heat. If griddle space permits, fry all 6 slices of egg-drenched bread, about 2–3 minutes per side, until golden brown. Or working in batches, use a skillet and fry 2 slices at a time (if working in batches, hold cooked French toast in a warm 250°F oven).

Taking 2 slices of the toast, smear the coconut cream cheese onto one side of the bread, forming a sandwich. Sprinkle with coconut flakes and a drizzle of maple syrup.

Grilled Cheese with Coconut Butter, Frisee, and Blood Orange

Makes 2 Sandwiches

During the winter months, indulging in a hearty slice of seed-studded whole bread—and the luscious combination of gruyere and fontina cheese—is only part of the act. The show stopper is the coconut butter. Unlike coconut oil, which is made from the extracted fat of coconut meat, coconut butter incorporates the fiber-rich coconut meat, in dried form. Exacting this goodness isn't an arduous task but does require just a pinch of patience and a 20-minute commitment to your food processor or Vitamix. The blood orange and frisee salad not only cuts the fat of the grilled cheese, but also offers a crisp, tart, toothsome bite, making this a very simple yet beautifully balanced meal.

2 cups shredded, unsweetened, coconut
4 slices seedy, whole grain bread
4 slices gruyere cheese
4 slices fontina cheese
3 blood oranges, 1 juiced and 2 segmented

1 tablespoon lemon juice
2 teaspoons honey
1 tablespoon extra-virgin olive oil
2 small heads frisee
Kosher salt and coarse ground black pepper

For the Coconut Butter: In a food processor, put the dried coconut and blend for 3 minutes until the coconut breaks down into clumps. Scrape down the sides of the food processor. Continue to blend for another 5 minutes and scrape down the sides of the food processor. The coconut should have a sandy consistency and be somewhat paste-like. Continue processing for another 3–4 minutes. Scrape sides of the food processor.

After 12–15 minutes have elapsed, the coconut starts to coagulate and it resembles a buttery paste. At this point, you should have scraped the sides of the food processor 6–7 times, to ensure that the coconut meat is making apt contact with the blades.

At the 20-minute mark, the coconut now resembles the consistency of thick peanut butter. Stir in the salt, and store refrigerated.

For the Grilled Cheese: Butter both sides of the bread with coconut butter. Divide the cheeses onto two slices of bread and close with another slice of coconut-buttered bread. Allow the sandwich to toast in a cast iron skillet over medium heat. When one side is golden brown and the cheese has started to melt, flip the sandwich. Remove from heat when both sides are crisp and golden and the cheese has melted.

For the Salad: Segment the blood oranges, firstly by removing the skin and pith and, with a paring knife, cutting the flesh out from along the veins of the fruit. Place the segments on a small plate. In a medium-sized bowl, juice the remaining blood orange by squeezing with your hand. To the blood orange juice, whisk in the lemon juice, honey, and slowly stream in the olive oil. Season to taste. Wash and trim the frisee into bite-sized pieces and toss in the blood orange vinaigrette. Top with orange segment and serve alongside grilled cheese sandwich.

Shrimp, Artichoke, and Saffron Risotto

Serves 4

When your calendar heralds the first day of winter, your kitchen should too.

1 teaspoon saffron threads

1¼ cups white wine, divided

1 pound large shrimp, peeled, deveined, shells reserved

1 large yellow onion, skin on, halved

2 teaspoons extra-virgin olive oil

Juice of 1 lemon

2 cloves garlic, minced

2 tablespoons butter, divided

1 large Vidalia onion, finely chopped, divided

6 baby artichokes, trimmed, halved; or 6 artichoke hearts, quartered

1 cup Arborio rice

½ cup parmesan cheese

¼ cut flat leaf parsley, chopped

In a small bowl, allow the saffron to bloom by incorporating it into ¼ cup of white wine. In a stock pot, bring 2 quarts of water, shrimp shells, and skin-on yellow onion to a boil. The skin of the onion imparts a yellow-ish incandescence to the stock, which shines through the rest of the meal. After 10 minutes, strain the stock, and place the pot back on the stove on low heat.

In a small bowl, combine the shrimp, olive oil, lemon juice, and garlic; marinate for 5–7 minutes.

In a large sauté pan, over medium-high heat, melt 1 tablespoon of butter and add half the Vidalia onions; sweat the onions, stirring regularly, until they are very tender, translucent, and fragrant. Add the shrimp and cook until they are opaque, about 3 minutes, then transfer the shrimp to a plate. Reserve the onions. Naturally, some of the onions will adhere to the shrimp. Fret not. Reduce heat to medium, add the artichokes to the pan, and sauté for about 10 minutes, stirring occasionally. When the artichokes begin to brown, remove from heat and place them on the same plate as the shrimp.

Increase the temperature to medium-high, add remaining butter and onions, and sauté until the onions are again tender, translucent, and very aromatic. Add the rice and stir continuously. Once the rice is emitting a slightly nutty aroma, cook for 5 more minutes. Add the white wine, including the wine used to bloom the saffron, to the toasted rice, and stir until all of the wine has been completely absorbed. Ladle in 1 cup of shrimp stock, and again, briskly stir until all has been absorbed. Continue this process, until the rice is cooked to al dente and not dry. If it appears to be too dry without any viscosity, add more stock, and stir until the stock is incorporated. Add the shrimp and artichokes back to the risotto, fold in the parmesan, season to taste, and serve immediately.

Shrimp Dumplings & Napa Cabbage Broth Bowl

Serves 4

Long before broth bowls were the flavor of the week, Asian soups were venerable culinary traditions for their healing power, sinus-clearing aromatics, and all-around nutritional oomph. Here, handmade dumplings occupy the lion's share of this broth bowl. And for a vegetarian alternative, nix the shrimp and replace with tofu, and the fish stock with vegetable stock. This rendition of a classic soup hones in on the power of some of the East's most enduring and healing properties.

1 pound shrimp (any size) peeled and deveined (shrimp shells reserved)

1 tablespoon ginger, grated and divided

4 cloves garlic, smashed

4 whole green onions, 2 stalks roughly chopped, 2 stalks bias cut

2 teaspoons sesame oil, divided

½ teaspoon red pepper flakes

1 large yellow onion, skin-on, quartered

36 round pre-packaged dumpling skins

1 quart shrimp stock

1 cup clam juice

¼ cup soy sauce

1 cup red onion, sliced

1 small Napa cabbage, halved, then thinly sliced lengthways

1 cup carrots, thinly bias cut

5 sprigs cilantro

1 teaspoon salt

1 teaspoon pepper

For the Dumplings: In a food processor, combine the shrimp, 1 tablespoon ginger, 2 cloves of garlic, rough chopped green onions, 1 teaspoon of sesame oil, and red pepper flakes. Pulse until the shrimp mixture forms a smooth paste. Line up dumpling skins on a clean work surface. Place a scant tablespoon of filling in the center of each skin. Employing a pastry brush, lightly moisten the edge of each dumpling skin with water. Following this, pinch the ends of the skins together to surround the filling. It should form a crescent shape. Continue this process until you have utilized all the filling. At the point, some of the dumplings can be frozen for use at another time.

For the Bowl: In a pot on medium-high heat, add 4 cups of water, the yellow onion, and the shrimp shells. Allow to simmer for 10 minutes. Strain and discard the shells and onion and reserve the liquid. Reduce heat to medium-low and to this shrimp stock add the clam juice, the remaining garlic and ginger, and soy sauce; bring to a very gently simmer. Add the shrimp dumplings and cook for about 3–5 minutes, until they begin to dance on the surface. At this point add in the red onion, carrots, bias cut scallions, and cabbage. Season to taste with salt and black pepper. Garnish with cilantro and a drizzle of sesame oil.

Blackened Shrimp Mac n' Cheese

Serves 4–6

It's impossible to calibrate the appeal and clamor of this perennial pasta dish. It's an all-ages, all-the-time workhorse of a meal that can be adapted in so many unique ways to satisfy a range of tastes. Here, extra-large shrimp are cooked in a simmer of sofrito, then melded with a combination of Cajun spices, then baked under a blanket of parmesan and sharp cheddar.

1½ pounds shrimp, peeled, deveined
1 tablespoon extra-virgin olive oil
4 cloves garlic, minced
1 medium yellow onion, diced
1 medium green + 1 red pepper,
   seeded, stemmed, diced
2 large tomatoes, medium diced

¼ cup cilantro, chopped
4 tablespoons butter, divided
1 pound elbow macaroni
2 cups extra-sharp cheddar, grated
½ cup parmesan cheese, grated
2 cups whole milk
¼ cup panko bread crumbs

For the Cajun Spice: Equal parts: salt, black pepper, garlic powder, paprika, onion powder, dried oregano, cayenne powder. Combine and toss the raw shrimp in the seasoning. Set aside.

For the Sofrito: Sauté the garlic and olive oil on medium heat until fragrant, about 2 minutes, then add the onion, peppers, and tomatoes, and cook for about 10 minutes. Add the cilantro. Using a hand-held blender or food processor, mince the sofrito to a semi-fine paste. Set aside ½ cup of sofrito and freeze the remainder. (Freezing sofrito in ice-cube trays makes easy work of starting soups, paellas, and other dishes.)

For the Mac n' Cheese: Bring a large stock pot of salted water to a boil. Add macaroni and cook until almost al dente, about 1–2 minutes less than the specified cooking time. Drain. Set aside.

Preheat oven to 350°F and butter a 9 × 13 baking dish.

In the sofrito pan, melt half the butter then add the shrimp. Add ½ cup of the sofrito mixture and cook on medium-high until the shrimp have just lost their blue color, since the cooking process will continue in the oven.

To the baking dish, mix together the pasta, cheddar, milk, and remaining butter. Stir in the shrimp mixture until very well combined. Top with the remaining ½ cup of cheese and panko. Bake for 35–40 minutes until the dish is bubbling and golden brown.

Blood Orange, Mint, and Ginger Margarita

Serves 4

If the punishing cold weather months have but one positive, it is the emergence of a bountiful crop of winter citrus. In this cocktail, the sweet sting of ginger is moderated by blood orange's acidic tang. And the familial bonds between agave and tequila offer both sweetness and intrigue. This is a full-flavored gem of a concoction, where all the elements detonate on your taste buds, resulting in a happily unexpected margarita, one which will leave you loving at least some aspects of winter.

1 cup 100% Blue Agave Tequila
½ cup blood orange juice (roughly 2–3 oranges), freshly squeezed
¼ cup lime juice
¼ cup agave nectar
8 large mint leaves
1 tablespoon fresh ginger root, grated
4 lime slices, to garnish

Place the mint and tequila in a Collins glass and macerate the leaves with a cocktail muddler. Set aside. Take a fine mesh sieve and place it over a small bowl and place the grated ginger root in the sieve. Using your fingers, press down on the ginger, extracting as much ginger juice as physically possible. Discard the now dry ginger. Next, using the same fine mesh sieve, strain the muddled mint and tequila into the bowl containing the ginger juice. Discard the mint.

In a cocktail shaker filled ¼ of the way with ice, add the ginger juice, mint, and tequila mixture. Next add the agave, lime juice, and blood orange juice. Shake vigorously. Pour into 4 rocks glasses and garnish with a slice of lime. Make another batch.

Clementine Honey Sparkler

Makes 4 Champagne Flutes

This cocktail is simple, refreshing, and dangerously unexpected. It is a welcomed change to the mimosa, with a subtle kick.

8 clementines, juiced

2 tablespoons raw honey

4 dashes Angostura bitters

¼ cup Grand Marnier

2 cups champagne

Stir to combine the clementine juice and honey, until the honey has dissolved. In a cocktail shaker with ice, combine the clementine honey mixture with the bitters and Grand Marnier. Shake well. Pour into chilled champagne flutes and top with champagne.

Ponche a Crème

Serves 4-6

In Trinidad & Tobago, there's a creamy type of clandestine Christmas punch that instantly turns Bah-Hum-Bug's into merry Ho-ho-ho's. Rum is melded with sweetened condensed milk, eggs, warm spices, and the indispensable Angostura bitters, to produce a heady drink that resembles eggnog but one that is more brazen and definitely more triumphant.

6 large eggs
Zest of 1 lime
3 (12-ounce) cans evaporated milk
2 (12-ounce) cans sweetened condensed milk
2 cups rum (light or dark)
1 teaspoon grated nutmeg
1 tablespoon Angostura bitters

In a large bowl, whisk the eggs and lime zest until frothy and very well combined, about 2 minutes. Next, add the evaporated milk and the condensed milk and stir until the milk and eggs are fully incorporated. Still stirring, with one hand, slowly stream in the rum and continue stirring for about another 2 minutes. Add in the nutmeg and Angostura bitters. Strain through a fine mesh sieve and transfer to an airtight container. Refrigerate immediately. Serve on the rocks with a sprinkle of nutmeg.

Champagne Ginger Sidecar

Makes 2

As with any good relic of history, the origins of the sidecar remain shrouded in mystery and intrigue. American barkeeps insist that the drink is the one happy product of prohibition. Meanwhile, our friends across the pond maintain it was invented in London at the end of World War I. Regardless of birthplace, the sidecar is beloved the world over for its ease, mitigated sweetness, and assertive citrus notes. Here, a touch ginger simple syrup and a cap of champagne makes magic of the most illusionary libation, the world over.

¼ cup Cointreau
¼ cup lemon juice
½ cup Cognac
¼ cup ginger simple syrup (page 50)
Champagne

In a cocktail shaker filled halfway with ice, combine the Cointreau, lemon juice, cognac, and simple syrup. Strain into a chilled rocks glass, top with champagne.

Triple Ginger-Ginger Snaps

Makes 2 dozen

The appeal of this cookie seldom crumbles, and multiple doses of the assertive namesake root give this crunchy little sweet treat all the oomph it deserves.

4 cups all-purpose flour
2 teaspoons baking soda
3 teaspoons cinnamon
2 teaspoons ground cloves
1 teaspoon ground nutmeg
1 teaspoon ground ginger powder
½ teaspoon salt

1¾ cups dark brown sugar
½ cup vegetable oil
⅔ cup molasses
1 large egg, room temperature
1 tablespoon fresh ginger, grated
½ teaspoon ginger extract
½ cup granulated sugar, for ganishing

Preheat oven to 350°F. Line a sheet pan with either parchment paper or a silpat. Sift together the flour, baking soda, cinnamon, cloves, nutmeg, ginger powder, and salt, in a large bowl. In an electric mixture using the paddle attachment, beat the brown sugar, oil, and molasses for about 3–5 minutes on medium-high. Turn to a very low speed, add the egg and beat until well combined, about 90 seconds. Add the fresh ginger. Scrape the bowl, beat for another 30 seconds, and very slowly add the dry ingredients. Increase to medium speed and beat for 3 minutes. Add the ginger extract and continue to mix for another 1–2 minutes until the dough is well combined. Scoop the dough and form small balls with your hands; flatten them lightly. Following this, press both sides of the cookie in the granulated sugar and place them on the sheet pans. Bake for 12–14 minutes and allow them to completely cool on a wire rack.

Rum-Laced Bundt Cake

Serves 6-8

Not too sweet, endlessly moist, and shamefully boozy. This joyful little bundt lives up to its name and guaranteed, it will be gone before you know it.

FOR THE CAKE
5 eggs
Rind of half a lime
1 cup dark rum
2 teaspoons vanilla extract
2½ cups cake flour
¾ cups brown sugar
¾ cups white sugar
2 teaspoons baking powder
1 teaspoon salt
1 teaspoon nutmeg
2 sticks butter, very soft

FOR THE GLAZE
1 stick butter
¼ cup water
1 cup white sugar
⅓ cup dark rum

Prepare the Cake: Preheat oven to 325°F. Heavily grease a bundt pan with butter, then add a light dusting of flour to the pan. Shake off excess flour. Set the pan aside.

In a medium-sized bowl, combine the eggs, lime rind, rum, and vanilla extract. Whisk to combine.

In the bowl of an electric mixer fitted with the paddle attachment, on low speed, add the cake flour, both sugars, baking powder, salt, and nutmeg. Mix on low for 1 minute to combine. Add the softened butter and allow the mixture to incorporate on medium-low speed, about 3 minutes. Remove the lime rind from the egg-rum mixture. Working in batches, add a bit of the egg-rum mixture to the dry ingredients. Ensure that the mixture is well-combined with the dry ingredients before adding more. Take note to scrape the sides of the bowl with a rubber spatula. Continue this process until all of the egg-rum mixture is utilized and the batter is smooth and well combined. Pour the batter into prepared bundt pan and bake for 60–70 minutes. Using a toothpick, check for doneness and allow the cake to cool on a wire rack.

For the Glaze: In a small saucepan over medium-high heat, melt the butter and water and sugar, and bring this to a boil, about 3–5 minutes. Reduce the heat to medium low and stir until the mixture has thickened, about 5 minutes. Remove from heat and add in the rum.

Using a toothpick or wooden skewer, poke holes all over the cake while it's still in the pan. Spoon half of the glaze over the cake and allow the glaze to seep in. Turn the cake onto the wire rack and continue to poke holes into it. Using a pastry brush, brush the remaining amount of glaze on the top and sides of the cake. If patience prevails, allow the cake to rest for 45 minutes prior to serving.

Boozy Coconut Bread Pudding

Serves 4-6

It may seem as if pies have monopolized the holiday dessert rotation, but here's an underdog of a contender eager to prove that day-old-bread, warm autumnal spices, eggs, sugar, and cream, could hold their own and maybe (just maybe) outbox the other sweet stalwarts.

6 eggs
1 cup sugar
1 teaspoon cinnamon
1 teaspoon nutmeg
½ teaspoon salt
1 (14-ounce) can coconut milk
1 cup heavy cream
1 tablespoon butter
8 cups day-old bread, cubed
¾ cups dark rum

In the bowl of an electric mixture with the whisk attached, combine the eggs, sugar, spices, and salt on medium-high speed for about 4 minutes until it is a little frothy. In a saucepan combine the coconut milk and heavy cream with the butter, and warm slightly. This cream mixture should not simmer or boil. Turn the mixer to low speed and slowly stream in the cream and coconut milk mixture, until it is well combined. Add the rum and turn the mixer to low speed.

   Preheat oven to 350°F and butter a 9×7 baking dish. Place the bread into the dish, then pour the custard over the bread. Using your hands, press the bread into the custard, ensuring that the bread is well absorbed. Bake for 45 minutes, or until the center of the pudding springs back when touched. Allow to cool for 10 minutes prior to serving.

EXTRAS

Brand-New for the Paperback Edition

Stew Peas

Serves 2-4

Jamaican stew peas are a star and staple of island cooking. Soaked in garlic and simmered with hefty aromatics and creamy coconut milk, this dish sizzles with bright bursts of deeply vegetal flavors. Even though this is a vegan dish, stew peas are a bold, meaty, one-pot dish that is at once light and satisfying.

14 ounces dried red kidney beans
11 large cloves garlic (5 whole, 6 minced), divided
6¼ cups water, divided
1 (13.5-ounce) can full-fat coconut milk
1 cup diced yellow onion
1 cup chopped scallions (about 5 stalks), plus more for garnish
1 large or 2 small carrots, diced
¼ cup fresh thyme leaves (about 1 bunch), chopped
½ Scotch bonnet (or habanero) pepper, seeded veins removed, finely chopped
2 tablespoons coconut oil
1 tablespoon kosher salt
1 teaspoon coarsely ground black pepper
1 teaspoon ground allspice
⅓ cup finely chopped red bell pepper
⅓ cup finely chopped green bell pepper
⅓ cup finely chopped yellow bell pepper
Cooked rice, for serving

The night before you plan to cook, sort through and rinse the red kidney beans. Place in a medium bowl and add 5 of the garlic cloves; pour in 6 cups of water. Cover and let stand at room temperature overnight.

The next day, transfer the beans, garlic, and soaking liquid to a large pot; add the coconut milk and bring to a rolling boil over high heat; reduce the heat to low, cover the pot, and simmer for 20 minutes (now is a good time to prep your aromatics and herbs).

Add the onion, scallions, carrots, thyme, minced garlic, and Scotch bonnet pepper. Stir to combine and continue to simmer on low until the red beans are soft and "break" when pressed with the back of a spoon, 20 to 25 minutes.

When the beans are tender, stir in ¼ cup water as well as the coconut oil. Stir in the salt, black pepper, and allspice. Remove the pot from the heat and stir in the bell peppers. Season to taste and serve over freshly cooked rice, garnished with more chopped scallions.

Callaloo

Serves 2-4

Callaloo in Trinidad and Tobago holds significant weight. It harkens back to a time—during the sixteenth to the nineteenth centuries—when enslaved Africans used plant life and ready aromatics to create a masterful meal out of seemingly nothing. Callaloo carries many variations. It's traditionally made with taro leaves (known as Xanthosoma in West Africa), okra, coconut milk, and a bevy of fresh aromatics. However, taro leaves can be difficult to source in the United States, so I've become accustomed to using a mix of spinach and collard greens in my adult rendering of this childhood staple. By incorporating collards into a dish that I've only known through the life and lens of my Caribbean, I'm giving the South its fair due, as well as giving tangible credence to our lives as islanders living in North Carolina. Pumpkin is also a central ingredient used in callaloo, although I've come to appreciate that the taste and texture of butternut squash lends for a strong enough proxy. Making this dish will always connect me to Trinidad and Tobago, but making it with the inclusion of some decidedly American ingredients most accurately reflects how truly nourishing and full of range cultural syncretism can be.

3 tablespoons vegetable oil
1 cup chopped yellow onion (about 1 small onion)
8 cloves garlic, minced
¾ cup chopped scallions (about 4 or 6 stalks)
1 cup chopped cilantro (about half a large bunch)
2 tablespoons fresh thyme leaves
1 bunch collard greens, well washed, chiffonade (about 1½ pounds)
4 cups baby spinach leaves, well washed
8 large okra pods, stems removed, sliced into small rounds
2 cups chopped butternut squash
1 (14-ounce) can full-fat coconut milk
1 tablespoon kosher salt
1 teaspoon coarse ground black pepper
½ teaspoon chopped habanero pepper, seeded and deveined
1 full habanero pepper

In a large stock pot over medium high heat, add the oil and heat for about 30 seconds. Next add the onions and garlic and sauté until fragrant and translucent, for about 1 minute. Add the scallions, cilantro, and thyme and sauté for another minute.

Add the collards and baby spinach to the aromatics, and stir to combine. Next add the okra, butternut squash, and coconut milk. Season with salt, pepper, and the chopped habanero pepper and stir to combine. Next add the whole habanero pepper and place on top of all the other ingredients. Reduce heat to medium low, cover, and simmer for 40 to 45 minutes. The butternut squash should be very tender and the greens thoroughly wilted.

Remove the full habanero pepper—it should be shriveled but still intact—and discard. Using a hand-held immersion blender, pulse the callaloo until the leaves and butternut squash are blended. If you don't have an immersion blender, use a countertop blender, working in batches. The mixture should be quite thick. Adjust seasoning if desired. Serve atop freshly steamed white rice.

Coconut Curried Shrimp

Serves 2-4

You'll be amazed at how just a handful of unsung ingredients can be transformed into a savory and satisfying meal that's signed, sealed, and delivered in under fifteen minutes. This dish sings with all of the namesake ingredients of this cookbook: coconut, ginger, and shrimp. It's a weekday workhouse that's easy to double, a leftover maven, and your new best friend.

¼ cup coconut oil
½ cup chopped white onion
2 tablespoons chopped garlic (about 6 cloves)
1 tablespoon chopped ginger (about 1 inch)
1 tablespoon madras curry powder
1 cup full-fat coconut milk
1 cup chopped scallions (about 5 stalks)
½ cup chopped cilantro
1 (15-ounce) can garbanzo beans, drained
1 pound shrimp, peeled and deveined
1 teaspoon salt
1 teaspoon coarse ground black pepper

In a medium sauté pan over medium-high heat, add the coconut oil and heat for 30 seconds. Then add the onions, garlic, and ginger, and sauté for another 30 seconds. Add the curry powder, stir to combine, and cook for 1 minute. Next, add the coconut milk, herbs, and garbanzo beans and cook for 5 minutes. Following this, add the shrimp and salt and pepper. Reduce heat to low, and simmer for 10 minutes. Serve with naan or with freshly steamed rice.

Spiked Lemon Lime & Bitters (LLB)

Serves 2-4

Born in the 1800s, Lemon Lime & Bitters is traditionally a non-alcoholic beverage and a staple of Australian golf culture, where it's enjoyed on the nineteenth hole. Over time the appeal of LLB grew and The House of Angostura in Trinidad and Tobago commercialized the drink with a ready-to-drink option. This version, spiked with rum, is tangy and nuanced with ever-present spice.

Juice and zest of 3 limes
Juice and zest of 3 lemons
¾ cup simple syrup
2 tablespoons Angostura bitters
1 (750 ml) bottle of San Pellegrino or other sparkling water
1 cup white rum

In a small bowl, steep the lime zest in the lime juice for 10 minutes. Repeat this process for the lemon zest and juice.

In a pitcher fitted with a small fine-mesh sieve, strain the lime juice and zest mixture, squeezing the pulp to ensure that all the liquid is removed from the zest. Repeat the process for the lemon.

Add the simple syrup, bitters, sparkling water, and rum. Stir to combine. Pour into an ice-filled highball glass and garnish with a slice of citrus.

Easy Citrusy Ginger Beer

Serves 2-4

Yes, ginger beer is typically fermented, but easy ginger beer with a distinct pucker of citrus is especially delightful and not to mention deliciously convenient.

1 pound ginger, washed and peeled
4 whole cloves
1 quart water, divided
Zest and juice of 3 limes
Zest and juice of 1 lemon
1½ cups granulated white sugar
1 tablespoon Angostura bitters
2 cups sparkling water

In a food processor or blender, pulse to mince the ginger and cloves with 1 cup of water. In a large bowl with a lid (or a pitcher with a lid), add the shredded ginger, cloves, lime zest and juice, lemon zest and juice, and sugar. Macerate using a muddler or a wooden spoon to get the juices flowing. Pour the remaining water over the ginger mixture. Cover and refrigerate for 24 hours.

Strain the liquid into another bowl or pitcher, pressing down on the ginger to ensure all the liquid is extracted. Add the bitters. Top with the sparkling water. Serve over ice with lime wedge garnish.

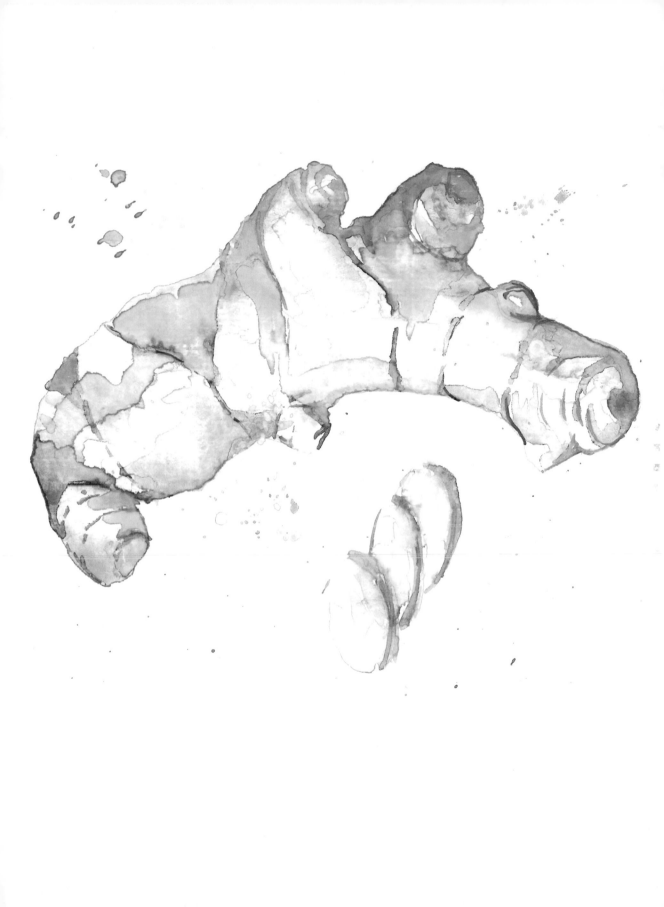

ACKNOWLEDGMENTS

There is one name on this cover, but behind that, there are so many others. My husband Joseph, thank you for being my loudest cheerleader and fiercest advocate. I love you with a loyalty that defies description. To Janice Shay, my fearless literary agent. You said "yes!" when everyone else gave me "no's." And to Leah Zarra, who edited this work in lightning speed and fierce accuracy. To Immanuel, for taking on an intensive photography project, in the middle of an already saturated life, and always coming to the shoots with an energy and excitement that I (still) envy. Thank you, Erin, for the incredible art work. And to my friends. To Kelly, Lauren, Dominic, Michelle (the coconut cake!) and Mark, the Father blessed me well with the gift of your friendship.

INDEX

CONVERSION CHARTS

METRIC AND IMPERIAL CONVERSIONS
(These conversions are rounded for convenience)

Ingredient	Cups/Tablespoons/ Teaspoons	Ounces	Grams/Milliliters
Butter	1 cup = 16 tablespoons = 2 sticks	8 ounces	230 grams
Cheese, shredded	1 cup	4 ounces	110 grams
Cream cheese	1 tablespoon	0.5 ounce	14.5 grams
Cornstarch	1 tablespoon	0.3 ounce	8 grams
Flour, all-purpose	1 cup/1 tablespoon	4.5 ounces/0.3 ounce	125 grams/8 grams
Flour, whole wheat	1 cup	4 ounces	120 grams
Fruit, dried	1 cup	4 ounces	120 grams
Fruits or veggies, chopped	1 cup	5 to 7 ounces	145 to 200 grams
Fruits or veggies, puréed	1 cup	8.5 ounces	245 grams
Honey, maple syrup, or corn syrup	1 tablespoon	0.75 ounce	20 grams
Liquids: cream, milk, water, or juice	1 cup	8 fluid ounces	240 milliliters
Oats	1 cup	5.5 ounces	150 grams
Salt	1 teaspoon	0.2 ounce	6 grams
Spices: cinnamon, cloves, ginger, or nutmeg (ground)	1 teaspoon	0.2 ounce	5 milliliters
Sugar, brown, firmly packed	1 cup	7 ounces	200 grams
Sugar, white	1 cup/1 tablespoon	7 ounces/0.5 ounce	200 grams/12.5 grams
Vanilla extract	1 teaspoon	0.2 ounce	4 grams

OVEN TEMPERATURES

Fahrenheit	Celsius	Gas Mark
225°	110°	¼
250°	120°	½
275°	140°	1
300°	150°	2
325°	160°	3
350°	180°	4
375°	190°	5
400°	200°	6
425°	220°	7
450°	230°	8